鋼の錬金術師

FULLMETAL ALCHEMIST

HIROMU ARAKAWA

荒川弘

22

■ アルフォンス・エルリック

Alphonse Elric

■ エドワード・エルリック

Edward Elric

■ アレックス・ルイ・アームストロング

Alex Louis Armstrong

■ ロイ・マスタング

Roy Mustang

OUTLINE
FULLMETAL ALCHEMIST

Using a forbidden alchemical ritual, the Elric brothers attempted to bring their dead mother back to life. But the ritual went wrong, consuming Edward Elric's leg and Alphonse Elric's entire body. At the cost of his arm, Edward was able to graft his brother's soul into a suit of armor. Equipped with mechanical "auto-mail" to replace his missing limbs, Edward becomes a state alchemist in hopes of finding a way to restore their bodies. Their search embroils them in a deadly conspiracy that threatens to take the innocence, if not the lives, of everyone involved.

As the "Day of Reckoning" approaches, an intricate chess game has emerged in Amestris. On one side stand the Elrics, Mustang's crew, Olivier Armstrong and a ragtag bunch of chimeras; on the other, Military Command, Kimblee, the Homunculi and their mysterious "Father." As our scattered heroes converge upon Central City, a dormant enemy steps up to stop them. To casual observers, Selim Bradley, the president's son, is the face of innocence. But behind that facade, he is the deadliest of the Homunculi—Pride—an amorphous mass of teeth and destruction.

鋼の錬金術師
FULLMETAL ALCHEMIST

▌CHARACTERS
FULLMETAL ALCHEMIST

■ ウィンリィ・ロックベル

Winry Rockbell

■ スカー

Scar

■ オリヴィエ・ミラ・アームストロング

Olivier Mira Armstrong

■ キング・ブラッドレイ

King Bradley

■ ヴァン・ホーエンハイム

Van Hohenheim

■ リン・ヤオ (グリード)

Lin Yao (Greed)

CONTENTS

MY PRINCE...

SORRY, HONEY.

I'M GREED.

WHA...

IN-COMING.

THAT'S ONE THING I CAN'T DO.

FOUL USURPER! GIVE MY PRINCE HIS BODY BACK!!

WHY DID YOU DO THAT?!

TMP

TMP

ANYONE CAN SEE THAT YOUR ARM HASN'T FULLY RE-COVERED.

WHAT DO YOU MEAN, "WHY?"

GREED CAN TAKE CARE OF HIMSELF!

SNIK

SLICE

AGH

MY ACTIONS ARE NOT YOUR CON-CERN!!

YOU SHOULD FOCUS ON PROTECTING YOURSELF!!

12

WHATEVER. JUST DON'T GO THROWING YOUR LIFE AWAY FOR NOTHING.

WE'RE GONNA NEED YOUR HELP LATER!!

THWACK

YEAH, I'LL MAN-AGE.

YOU ALL RIGHT, HEINKEL?

LION GUY!

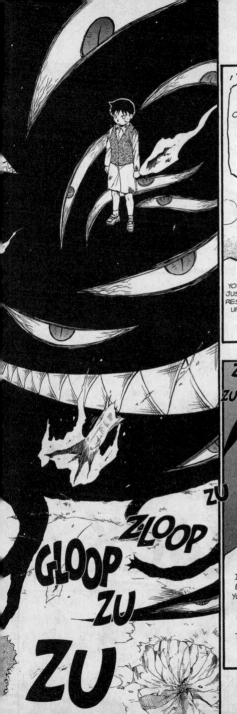

SORRY. I COULDN'T FINISH HIM OFF.

DON'T WORRY A-BOUT IT. YOU JUST REST UP.

ZU
ZU

ZU

ZLOOP

GLOOP ZU

ZU

I CAN'T BLAME YOU FOR NOT BEING ABLE TO KILL IT.

14

MUNCH

MUNCH

MUNCH

MUNCH

ZU ZU ZU

EVEN TO ME, THAT THING IS A MONSTER.

17

W-WHERE AM I?

THE KANAMA SLUMS, ON THE OUTSKIRTS OF CENTRAL CITY.

GRAB YOUR STUFF!

HOW DID I GET HERE?

GET ALL THE MEN!

GET A BUCK-ET!!

THAT'S DAR-IUS.

I KNOW.

GORIUS TOLD ME.

SELIM BRADLEY IS A HOMUN-CULUS!!

OH!! DAD!!

HRM...

THERE THEY ARE.

RSTL

RSTL

OH!

I SEE... THE HOMUNCULI ARE ESSENTIALLY DERIVED FROM MY BODY...

PERHAPS IT'S EASIER TO CONTROL YOU BECAUSE YOU SHARE MY BLOOD.

I FEEL DIRTY. THAT THING HAD ITS TENDRILS INSIDE ME, AND ITS SPIRIT WAS CONTROLLING ME.

UGH...

YOU OK?!

OW OW OW!!

FIRST, WE NEED TO TREAT HIS WOUNDS. WE'LL TALK LATER.

OLD MAN FOO!

AND JUDGING FROM YOUR APPEARANCE, YOU MUST BE FROM...XING?

SO YOU'RE EDWARD'S FATHER.

WHAT ARE WE GONNA DO ABOUT THAT SHADOW MONSTER?

HEY! THIS IS NO TIME FOR CHATTING!

WHAT A WONDERFUL COUNTRY. LONG AGO, WHEN I—

THAT'S RIGHT.

SHADOW?

IT ATE THAT THING CALLED GLU...SOMETHING AND NOW WE CAN'T EVEN GET CLOSE TO IT.

THAT'S RIGHT.

YOU MEAN PRIDE, THE HOMUNCULUS?

FOOM

FOOM
FOOM

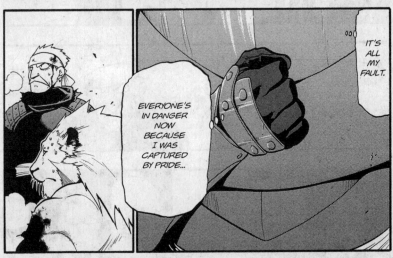

IT'S ALL MY FAULT.

EVERYONE'S IN DANGER NOW BECAUSE I WAS CAPTURED BY PRIDE...

IF WE DON'T FIGURE SOMETHING OUT SOON, THOSE VILLAGERS ARE GOING TO GET THEMSELVES KILLED.

UH-OH.

WUZA WUZA

THERE'S NO WAY WE CAN USE THE SAME PLAN AGAIN.

THE FIRE IS CREATING A LIGHT SOURCE, AND I'VE USED UP ALL MY FLASH BOMBS.

20

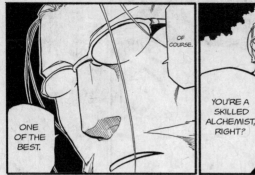
OF COURSE.

ONE OF THE BEST.

DAD.

YOU'RE A SKILLED ALCHEMIST, RIGHT?

GOOD, BECAUSE I HAVE A PLAN THAT'S GOING TO TAKE A MAJOR FEAT OF ALCHEMY TO PULL OFF.

KA-

THUNK

KREEEAK

WITH NOTHING LEFT TO OBSTRUCT MY VIEW...

MUCH BETTER.

SNAK SNIK CRACK

SO...

SNIF SNIF

YOU'VE FINALLY DECIDED TO SHOW YOURSELF...

!

TCH

...I WONDER HOW MUCH LONGER GREED WILL SURVIVE?

YOUR SMELL GIVES YOU AWAY.

AND THERE'S NO USE IN HIDING BEHIND OBJECTS, EITHER.

ZLOOP

THE HERO ALWAYS ARRIVES FASHION-ABLY LATE.

HOHEN-HEIM!

YUP.

SNAP

IF YOU'RE THE "HERO," DOES THAT MEAN YOU PLAN ON DEFEATING ME?

NOT AT ALL! THAT'S IMPOSSIBLE.

HA HA HA!

SHF

SHF

I'M NOT THAT BRAVE.

I HAVE NO INTENTION OF FIGHTING YOU.

23

HE MUST BE PLOTTING SOMETHING...

WHAT COULD HE BE THINKING?

...

ZWU...

WILL THEY TRY TO DIMINISH MY STRENGTH WITH ANOTHER FLASH BOMB?

ZU ZU ZU

SHF

JUST A LITTLE MORE... A BIT MORE TOWARDS THE CENTER...

GOOD.

IT'S CONCENTRATING ITS SHADOWS AROUND THE BOY IN ORDER TO FOCUS MY ATTENTION IN ONE PLACE.

24

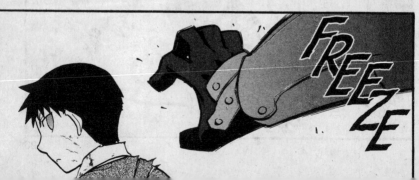

ZU

ZU ZU ZU ZU

ZU ZU

ZU ZU

KREEE

ZWU ZWU ZWU

THAT'S IT? FOCUS MY ATTENTION ON HOHENHEIM, THEN STRIKE WHEN MY GUARD IS DOWN?

WHAT A PITIFULLY SIMPLE PLAN.

OH!

BUT IF I EXTEND MY LINE TOO FAR, YOU'LL HIT ME WITH A FLASH BOMB.

KREE- KREE- SQUEE

ZWU

ZWOO ZWOOP

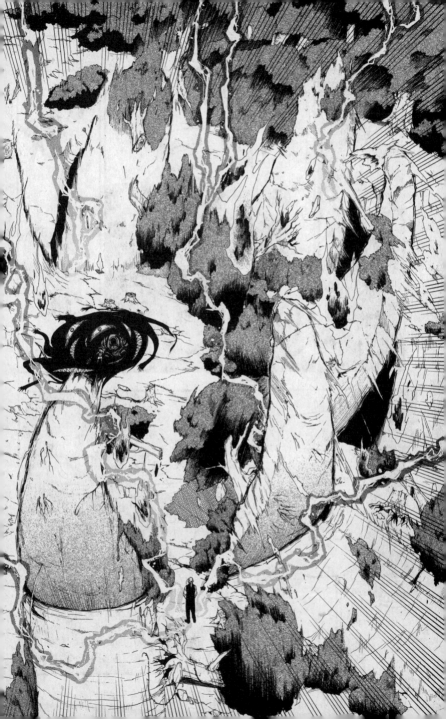

THAT WAS SCARY...

BA-DUM BA-DUM

WOW! YOU'RE AMAZING!

TONK TONK

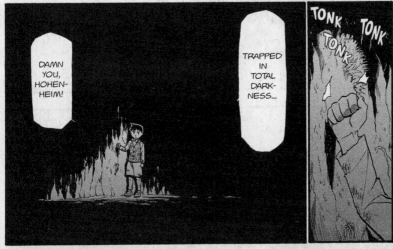

DAMN YOU, HOHEN-HEIM!

TRAPPED IN TOTAL DARK-NESS...

TONK TONK

TONK

SO YOU'RE TRAPPED IN HERE AS WELL.

THAT'S ALPHONSE ELRIC'S VOICE...

YOUR POWERS ARE USE-LESS IN HERE.

HA HA HA MY PLAN WORK-ED!

32

THIS IS NO TIME FOR LAUGHTER.

THE MOMENT YOU MAKE AN OPENING TO GET OUT, I'LL USE MY SHADOW TO—

I NEVER HAD ANY INTENTION OF GETTING OUT OF HERE.

I MEAN...

...PRIDE THE HOMUNCULUS.

NOW WE'LL SEE WHO CAN MAINTAIN THEIR PATIENCE THE LONGEST, SELIM...

MAYBE WE SHOULD STAY HERE UNTIL YOUR SO-CALLED "PROMISED DAY" HAS PASSED US BY.

MY BODY DOESN'T REQUIRE OXYGEN, LIGHT OR FOOD.

HOW ABOUT YOU, OLD MAN?

I'M FINE, SIRE...

HOW'S HEINKEL DOING?

HUGE...

HIS WOUNDS HAVE BEEN TREATED, SIRE.

...

GOOD, GOOD.

AND YOU SEEM ALL RIGHT TOO, LITTLE LADY.

MIND YOUR OWN BUSINESS, I'M FINE!!

BUT YOU'RE GREED RIGHT NOW, AREN'T YOU?

WHAT'S THE MEANING OF THIS?!

HEY, HOHEN-HEIM!

WHAT'S GOING ON?!

IT WAS AL'S IDEA.

WHA...?

WHAT THE HELL WERE YOU THINK-ING?!

AL'S TRAPPED IN THERE WITH THAT MONSTER!

BECAUSE AL SAID, "IF YOU TELL BIG BROTHER, HE'LL BE AGAINST THE PLAN FOR SURE."

SINCE WE CAN'T DEFEAT IT, OUR BEST OPTION WAS TO IMPRISON IT.

AND IF WE TRIED, THERE'S NO TELLING HOW MANY INNOCENTS WOULD HAVE DIED IN THE CROSS FIRE.

DEFEATING PRIDE IN ITS PRESENT STATE IS NEAR IMPOS-SIBLE.

BUT WHY DIDN'T YOU AT LEAST CONSULT WITH ME BEFORE YOU—

NOW WE'VE BOUGHT OURSELVES SOME TIME TO COME UP WITH A MORE *PERMANENT* WAY OF DEALING WITH PRIDE.

AL VOLUNTEERED BECAUSE HE KNEW HE WAS THE ONE THAT WAS MOST SUITED FOR THE TASK.

IN ORDER TO TRAP PRIDE, WE HAD TO MAKE SURE IT GATHERED AS MUCH OF ITS SHADOW AS POSSIBLE TOWARDS THE CENTER.

OR ELSE AL'S GONNA BE ROASTED ALIVE.

ALL RIGHT THEN, LET'S PUT THIS FIRE OUT.

HE CAME UP WITH A PLAN THAT WOULD ALLOW ALL OF US TO SURVIVE.

HUH?

HM?

DAMN IT...

GIVE IT UP.

DAD WOULDN'T HAVE MADE THE WALL SO WEAK THAT IT COULD BE DUG THROUGH BY A CHILD.

IT WON'T WORK.

ARE YOU TRYING TO DIG YOUR WAY OUT?

?!

KLATANK

FWUMP

TRIP

I TRIPPED ON IT AND FELL.

STUPID HEAD!

UH...

HUH ?!

ARE YOU LAUGHING AT ME?

NOW THAT HE'S LOST ALL HIS POWERS, HE'S NOTHING BUT A CHILD...

IS THIS REALLY THAT SAME TERRIFYING HOMUNCULUS?

NOT AT ALL.

SHE'S JUST A HUMAN LIVING IN BLISSFUL IGNORANCE.

WAIT!! IS SHE IN ON IT TOO ?!

AFTER ALL, YOU EVEN FOOLED MRS. BRADLEY...

I WAS JUST THINKING THAT IF IT WEREN'T FOR YOUR POWERS AS A HOMUNCULUS, YOU'D BE A PERFECTLY REGULAR KID. IT WOULD BE REALLY EASY TO BE DECEIVED BY YOUR APPEARANCE.

WELL...

HOW COULD YOU?! SHE'S SUCH A NICE PERSON !!

I BET YOU WERE MOCKING HER BEHIND HER BACK!

THEN YOU WERE DECEIVING HER!

40

I GUESS SHE'S REALLY THE EPITOME OF A "GOOD MOTHER."

THAT'S TRUE.

ONCE WHEN I WAS ALMOST RUN OVER BY A CAR, SHE PUT HERSELF IN HARM'S WAY TO SAVE ME.

I WAS TRULY SHOCKED BY HER SELFLESS-NESS.

OF COURSE, I COULD'VE EASILY SAVED MYSELF IF I HAD WANTED TO...

I'VE ALWAYS HAD A FATHER, BUT NEVER A MOTHER. I WAS HONESTLY... INTRIGUED.

I THOUGHT TO MYSELF... "SO THIS IS WHAT A MOTHER IS LIKE."

TONNG
TONNG

TONNG

MAYBE WE WERE ONLY *PRETENDING* TO BE A *FAMILY,* BUT I DO HAVE AFFECTION FOR HER.

THAT'S THE TRUTH.

UH...

I...I KNOW YOU GUYS NEED US AS HUMAN SACRIFICES !!

UH... UM....

HEY !!

DON'T BE FOOLED !

42

SO DON'T YOU THINK YOUR PLANS WERE A BIT FLAWED?

IF WE HAD LEFT THE COUNTRY IN ORDER TO SAVE OUR OWN LIVES, ALL OF YOUR PLANS WOULD'VE BEEN FOR NOTHING, RIGHT?

YOU HAD NO INTENTION OF SAVING ONLY YOURSELVES. ON THE CONTRARY, YOU CAME TO US IN CENTRAL CITY TO FIGHT.

BUT ALL OF YOU *DID* REMAIN IN THIS COUNTRY.

THAT'S HOW YOU HUMAN BEINGS ARE.

WE SIMPLY SELECTED THOSE OF YOU WHO POSSESSED THAT QUALITY IN ABUNDANCE.

IF THERE IS ONE THING YOUR KIND HAVE SHOWN US OVER THE CENTURIES, IT'S HOW PREDICTABLE THE HUMAN SPIRIT IS.

IT'S HARD TO KNOW WHETHER HE'S PRAISING US OR MOCKING US...

SO THEN...

HA HA

OH!!

HUH?

KLATA
RSTL
SHVE
KLUNK
KLATA

I THOUGHT YOU'D BEEN CAPTURED BY THE MILITARY.

HEY, ISHBALAN GUY, LONG TIME NO SEE!

KLATTA

YOU KNOW, THE ONE WITH THE BLACK-AND-WHITE CAT.

HUH? WHERE'S THE LITTLE GIRL?

HUH?

IT'S PRACTICALLY IN THE FOREST.

IT'S IN THE SOUTHERN OUTSKIRTS OF CENTRAL.

YEAH, IT'S HARD TO FIND.

I'M LOOKING FOR THE KANAMA DISTRICT.

WHAT?!

SHE CAME BACK HERE A LITTLE WHILE AGO. ASSUMED SHE WAS STILL WITH YOU.

45

WHAT THE HECK IS SHE DOING HERE?

SHE DIDN'T GO BACK TO HER COUNTRY?

WHAT?!

BUT I'M SURE YOU ALREADY KNEW ABOUT THAT, RIGHT?

I HEARD THAT PRESIDENT BRADLEY DIED WHEN HE WENT EAST.

OH!

LET'S SEE...

WHAT'S BEEN GOING ON?

WE'VE BEEN OUT OF THE LOOP FOR A WHILE.

UH-HUH.

WE JUST ASSUMED THAT...

I DON'T THINK SO.

HUH? WASN'T IT THE ISHBALANS WHO DID IT?

THAT'S THE FIRST TIME I'VE HEARD ABOUT IT!

IT'S TRUE THAT THERE ARE MANY ISHBALANS COMING TO THE CITY, BUT THAT'S NOT WHAT THEY'RE HERE FOR.

WORD AROUND TOWN IS THAT THEY'RE PLANNING SOME KIND OF **TERRORIST ACTIVITY.**

IT'S JUST THAT...

... LOTS OF ISHBALANS HAVE BEEN COMING HERE TO CENTRAL CITY OVER THE LAST FEW DAYS.

...WITHOUT RE-SORTING TO TERROR-ISM.

THEY ARE VALUABLE ALLIES WHO HAVE COME HERE TO BRING CHANGE...

KLAK

KLAK

KLAK

KLAK

I'VE STAINED MY BRAND-NEW SUIT.

KLAK

OH, WHAT A SHAME.

FULLMETAL
ALCHEMIST

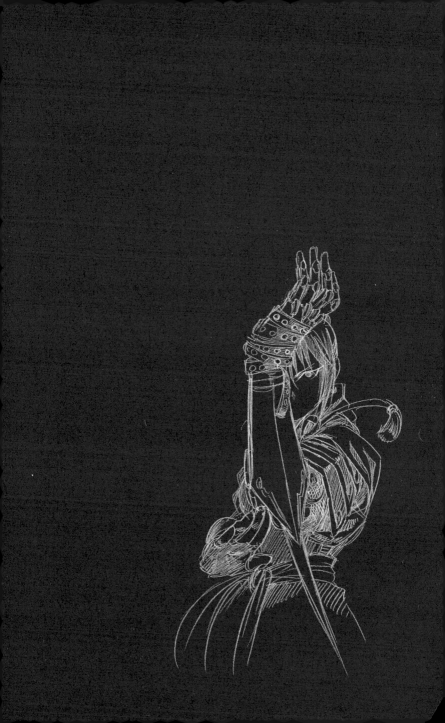

WHAT HAP- PENED HERE ?

WAS IT A FIRE ?

WHOA. WHAT'S THIS ?

THESE ARE THE KANAMA SLUMS, RIGHT?

AND WHAT'S UP WITH THAT WEIRD MOUN- TAIN?

JELSO AND ZANPANO!

HEY!! DARIUS?!

HUH? HUH? HUH?

I QUIT WORKING FOR KIMBLEE AGES AGO!

WHAT ARE YOU TALK-ING ABOUT?

YOU BASTARD, DID KIMBLEE SEND YOU HERE TO FINISH US OFF?!

GYA! YADDA! BICKER!

IRK! GYA!

...AND SCAR...

YOU IDIOTS! LISTEN TO WHAT I'M TELLING YOU!!

RAAH! SQUABBLE!

YOU'RE JUST TRYING TO TRICK US SO YOU CAN KILL US WITH THAT SAW, AREN'T YOU?!!

GYA!

OH HEY! DR. MARCOH!

EDWARD!

YOU WANNA MESS WITH US, SHORTY?!!

PIGGY, FATTY, AND GORILLA, STOP FIGHTING.

SHUT UP.

THAT'S TRUE.

IT WAS PRETTY OBVIOUS THAT HE WAS GONNA DUMP US AS SOON AS HE GOT WHAT HE NEEDED.

THERE WAS NO POINT IN WORKING FOR A GUY LIKE THAT.

UH-HUH.

WHAT? YOU GUYS TOO?

AT THE VERY LEAST, THOSE GUYS WILL NEVER ABANDON US.

YUP.

AFTER ESCAPING FROM KIMBLEE WE BECAME FUGITIVES, BUT HEY, NO REGRETS, EH?

HUH?

BY HIM-SELF?

HE WENT TO CHECK OUT WHAT'S HAPPENING INSIDE CENTRAL CITY.

WHERE'S THE OLD MAN GOING?

HE SAID THAT HIS FACE IS THE ONLY ONE THAT'S NOT KNOWN TO THE ENEMY, SO IT'S EASIER.

...BUT I'M SURE HE'S MAINLY WORRIED ABOUT LIN'S WHERE-ABOUTS.

HE ALSO SAID HE WOULD TRY TO FIND OUT WHAT COLONEL MUSTANG IS UP TO AS MUCH AS POSSIBLE...

OH, OKAY...

UH-HUH...

ARE YOU FINISHED TALKING TO SCAR AND THE OTHERS?

WE'RE ALL SET THEN.

I'D GO CRAZY IF I WAS STUCK IN TOTAL DARKNESS WITH A MONSTER LIKE THAT.

TELL ME A-BOUT IT.

YOUR BROTHER SURE IS SOME-THING ELSE.

THE REST...

POF

POF

AL IS GOING ABOVE AND BEYOND TO KEEP US SAFE.

...IS UP TO US.

Chapter 89
Soldiers' Return

A SOLAR ECLIPSE?

WELL, I GUESS YOU COULD PUT SOME SOOT ON THE LENS...

THEN WHAT SHOULD WE DO?

OH, OKAY.

GASP!!

NO WAY!!

IF YOU LOOK AT THE SUN WITH A TELESCOPE, YOU'LL GO BLIND.

UH, GUYS...

?

58

LOOK, BIG BROTH-ER!

?!

TMp TMp TMp TMp

HEY, DENNY. YOU KNOW YOU'RE TOO LATE FOR BREAKFAST, RIGHT?

I DON'T WANT ANY!

BIG BROTH-ER?

YOU GUYS, DON'T GO OUTSIDE TODAY.

FOUR, SIR— COLONEL MUSTANG, LT. HAWKEYE, 2ND LT. BREDA AND SGT. MAJOR FURY.

HOW MANY OF THEM ARE THERE?

THAT FOOL DOESN'T KNOW WHEN TO QUIT.

HE COULD HAVE KEPT HIS PRECIOUS SUBORDINATES IF HE HAD JUST DONE AS HE WAS TOLD.

KLAK

KLAK

THAT DOESN'T MATTER.

WE'RE UNABLE TO RETALIATE BECAUSE THEY'VE TAKEN THE PRESIDENT'S WIFE HOSTAGE, SIR.

DON'T WORRY ABOUT THE PRES-IDENT'S WIFE.

KLAK

KLAK

KLAK

SIR?

THE PRES-IDENT'S WIFE IS USELESS TO US.

JUST MAKE SURE YOU CAPTURE ROY MUSTANG *ALIVE*.

62

TMP TMP TMP
TMP TMP

THIS WAY!!

HURRY!!

C3! CHECK UP TOP!

THEY'VE GOT THE PRESIDENT'S WIFE WITH THEM!

C6! GUARD THE EXIT!

THEY WON'T GET FAR!

YOU CAN'T USE YOUR FLAMES IN THESE CLOSE QUARTERS, CAN YOU, TRAITOR?

65

YOU WON'T SHOOT, NOT WITH HER HERE.

SHOOT EVERY-ONE...

...EXCEPT COLONEL MUSTANG.

CHAK

BLAM BLAM BLAM BOOM

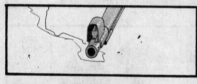

BULL'S EYE.

TOK

HUH ?

EVERYONE EXCEPT THE COLONEL? SO YOU WERE GONNA SHOOT THE PRESIDENT'S WIFE TOO?

BUT NOW I WISH I HADN'T.

THOSE WERE THE WORDS I WANTED TO HEAR...

CAN IT BE...?

...BEEN ABANDONED BY THIS COUNTRY?

HAVE MY HUSBAND AND I...

ARE THESE GUYS NUTS?

GUNNING DOWN AWOL SOLDIERS LIKE US, I GET, BUT THE PRESIDENT'S WIFE?!

...WAS IT MY HUSBAND WHO ABANDONED ME?

OR...

I DON'T KNOW, BUT I PROMISE THAT WE WILL PROTECT YOUR LIFE NO MATTER WHAT.

I DON'T KNOW, MA'AM.

AND WHEN ALL OF THIS IS OVER, YOU CAN PROVE TO THE GOOD PEOPLE OF THIS NATION THAT WE WEREN'T THE ONES WHO CROSSED THE LINE.

70

MAYBE WE COULD MOVE FASTER IF SHE WAS UNCONSCIOUS, SIR.

IF SHE PASSES OUT, OUR MOVEMENT WILL BE HINDERED EVEN FURTHER.

NO.

YOU HAVEN'T TOLD THE PRESIDENT'S WIFE THAT HER HUSBAND IS MISSING YET?

YOU SURE ARE POPULAR, COLONEL.

THERE ARE TROOPS ALL OVER THE PLACE, SIR.

KRAKLE

THE OTHERS WILL BE MAKING THEIR MOVE RIGHT ABOUT NOW.

LURE THEM IN AS CLOSE AS POSSIBLE.

BZZT

71

72

73

74

ZERO CA-SUAL-TIES!

FIVE IN-JURED!

WHAT'S OUR DAM-AGE?!

CRAP! I'VE BLOWN MY EARDRUM!

I THOUGHT I WAS GONNA DIE!

GEHOFF

RE-TREAT!

...!

WE'RE LUCKY NO ONE DIED.

KA- BLAM

...DON'T YOU THINK IT'S ODD THAT WE DON'T HAVE ANY CASUAL-TIES?

CON-SIDERING THAT THEY HAVE "THE HERO OF ISHBAL" AND THE INFAMOUS "HAWKEYE"...

COULD IT BE...?

IT MUST BE TRUE. THEY'RE...

GAAGH!

NO, SIR.

THEY'RE NOT KILLING ANYONE ?!

CLENCH

SEND OUT BOTH THE DIMITRI AND KIM SQUADS !!

I WANT TO SEE THE CORPSES OF MUSTANG'S MEN STACKED UP RIGHT HERE IN FRONT OF ME!!

TH...

THEY'RE MOCKING US!

MANY HAVE BEEN WOUNDED, BUT SO FAR WE'VE SUFFERED ZERO CASUAL-TIES.

EVEN THE MEN WHO HAVE BEEN SHOT HAVE ALL BEEN WOUNDED IN NONVITAL AREAS OF THEIR BODIES.

76

DON'T LET THEM GET IN **HIS** WAY!!

WHAT THE HELL IS BRIGADIER GENERAL KLEMIN DOING?!

MUSTANG STILL HASN'T BEEN CAPTURED?

THERE'S NO WAY THEY CAN KEEP THAT UP.

I HEAR THAT THE ENEMY IS DIMINISHING OUR COMBAT STRENGTH WITHOUT EVEN KILLING ANY OF OUR TROOPS...

WHAT IS HE THINKING?

QUITE SO.

COLO-NEL MUSTANG MUST HAVE GONE SOFT.

THIS IS ALL MERE *CHILD'S PLAY*.

BUT THE CENTRAL CITY TROOPS MUST BE *EVEN SOFTER* IF THEY CAN'T DEFEAT THEM.

...BUT THAT OVER-CONFI-DENCE IS THIS COUNTRY'S BIGGEST WEAKNESS.

YOU COULD THANK THE MAN DOWNSTAIRS FOR KEEPING OUR BORDERS SAFE BY STAYING ON THE OFFEN-SIVE...

SINCE ITS FOUNDING, THIS COUNTRY HAS NEVER BEEN ATTACKED BY A POWERFUL ENEMY.

WHAT?

YOU FORGET YOUR PLACE, ARMSTRONG.

THEREFORE, HOW ABOUT LENDING ME A FEW OF YOUR CENTRAL CITY TROOPS?

YOU'RE GREAT AT ATTACKING BUT HAVE A TERRIBLE DEFENSE.

DO YOU REALLY THINK YOU'RE HERE BECAUSE OF YOUR ABILITIES?

YOU'RE MERELY BEING *DETAINED* HERE, THAT'S ALL.

PLUS, YOU SAW THE TROOPS THAT WE HAVE STORED UNDER-GROUND, DIDN'T YOU?

KEEP THEM IN MIND IF YOU HAVE ANY IDEAS OF REBELLION.

HA HA HA!

I'M AWARE OF THE CLOSE BOND BETWEEN YOU AND YOUR BRIGGS TROOPS.

KEEPING YOU HERE ACTS AS A POWERFUL DETERRENT AGAINST THE THREAT OF RESISTANCE FROM THOSE MEN.

"SURVIVAL OF THE FITTEST" IS THE LAW OF BRIGGS!!

IF I DIED HERE, THEY WOULD SIMPLY CAST ME ASIDE BECAUSE I WAS TOO WEAK.

I'VE ALREADY TOLD MY MEN TO ABANDON ME IN THE EVENT OF AN EMERGENCY.

YOU UNDERSTAND *NOTHING* ABOUT US.

WHAT?!

THAT'S THE BRIGGS ARMY.

A FORCE THAT CAN ACT UNFLINCHINGLY AND WITHOUT HESITATION EVEN IN MY ABSENCE...

TMP
TMP

TMP
TMP

WE CAN FINALLY SAY GOODBYE TO THIS UNDERGROUND STORAGE.

TMP
TMP

ALL RIGHT.

LET'S GO.

COLONEL MUSTANG IS ENGAGED IN COMBAT IN THE WESTERN INDUSTRIAL SECTOR.

A LARGE NUMBER OF ENEMY TROOPS HAVE BEEN SENT THERE.

DON'T TALK SO LIGHTLY ABOUT THE TROOPS THAT I'VE TRAINED WITHOUT KNOWING THE FACTS.

IT'S TIME TO RIP OUT THE THROATS OF THOSE SPINELESS FOOLS IN CENTRAL CITY HEADQUARTERS.

TMP
TMP
TMP
TMP
TMP

VETERANS, ALL. EACH ONE OF THEM CAPABLE OF GOING TOE-TO-TOE WITH A BRIGGS MOUNTAIN GRIZZLY.

WOOO
WOOO
?!
SEE? HERE THEY COME NOW.

WOOO WOO

THOSE DOLLS THAT YOU'RE ALL SO PROUD OF VERSUS MY MEN— I WONDER WHICH WILL PROVE TO BE STRONGER?

HOW CAN THAT BE? IT'S NOT LIKE THEY CAN USE MAGIC!!

THEY JUST SPRANG UP INSIDE THE CITY OUT OF NOWHERE...

WOOOO

MORE TROOPS ?!

WOOO

HOW MANY MEN DO THEY HAVE ?!

UN- KNOWN, SIR! BUT JUDGING FROM THEIR EQUIP- MENT THEY MUST BE...

DAMMIT! OF ALL THE PLACES THEY COULD'VE STRUCK, THEY HAD TO ATTACK US IN THE WESTERN SECTOR WHERE WE HAVE SO FEW MEN...

WOOO WOOO

UNBE- LIEVABLE! WHERE DID THEY COME FROM?!!

82

...FROM THE NORTH—

SHUNK

JUST HOW BIG IS THAT MANSION ANYWAY, SIR?!

WE SNUCK IN WEAPONS AND TROOPS BY HIDING THEM AMONGST THE CONSTRUCTION SUPPLIES WHILE THE MANSION WAS UNDER REPAIR.

UH-HUH.

INSIDE THE ARM-STRONG MAN-SION?!

RA-TA TAT TAT

STOP LYING. YOU KNOW YOU WOULD NEVER KILL YOURSELF.

I'M DOWN TO MY LAST BULLET, AND I GOTTA SAVE THAT ONE FOR ME.

DAMMIT! ALMOST EVERY-ONE'S OUT OF AMMO NOW.

KLINK

CHARLIE, TOSS ME A CLIP!

SKKID

PLUS, I HAVE A WIFE WHO'S WAITING FOR ME AT HOME.

I DON'T WANT TO DIE WITH ANOTHER MAN, SIR.

UM... ISN'T THAT WHERE YOU'RE SUPPOSED TO SAY, "I'LL STAY WITH YOU TILL THE BITTER END, SIR"?

HEY, YOU TWO. DON'T HESITATE TO LEAVE ME BEHIND AND ESCAPE IF THERE'S NO OTHER CHOICE.

ROGER THAT!

OH, IS THAT SO?!

KOFF

GAGH!

GEHOFF

KOFF KOFF

84

89

90

THANK YOU VERY MUCH FOR—

THIS IS COLONEL MUSTANG FROM THE STATE MILITARY SPEAKING.

AN IMPORTANT OFFICIAL FROM XING?

HERE YOU GO, SIR.

PFT!

HEH HEH HEH...

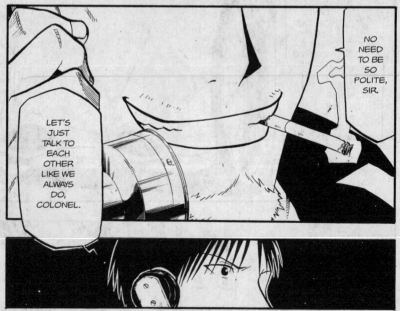

NO NEED TO BE SO POLITE, SIR.

LET'S JUST TALK TO EACH OTHER LIKE WE ALWAYS DO, COLONEL.

WELL, SIR?

I'LL PAY YOU WHEN I'M PROMOTED.

PUT IT ON MY TAB!

HOW WOULD YOU LIKE TO PAY?

FULLMETAL
ALCHEMIST

Chapter 90
Army of Immortals

FULLMETAL
ALCHEMIST

SHE'S RIGHT.

I CAN FAINTLY HEAR A SIREN TOO.

WHAT ?

THERE'S SMOKE RISING FROM THE CITY.

OKAY.

I SAY WE TAKE ADVANTAGE OF THE COMMOTION AND STRIKE AT THE CENTER OF THE UNDER-GROUND PASSAGE-WAYS.

I DO HAVE A COUNTER-MEASURE IN CASE HE ACTIVATES THE NATIONAL TRANSMUTATION CIRCLE, BUT IF WE CAN PREVENT HIM FROM ACTIVATING IT, THAT WOULD BE IDEAL.

THEY MUST BE REALLY GOING WILD THEN.

SO THE COLONEL AND THE OTHERS ARE MAKING THEIR MOVE?

WHAT'RE WE GONNA DO?

99

IF WE DESTROY THE CONTAINER, HE'LL MOST LIKELY DIE.

HE'S STILL THE SAME DWARF INSIDE THE FLASK. HE'S JUST GOTTEN BIGGER, THAT'S ALL.

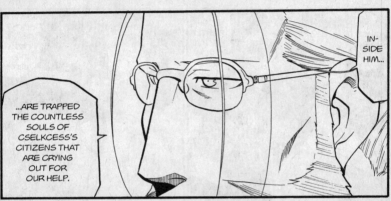

IN-SIDE HIM...

...ARE TRAPPED THE COUNTLESS SOULS OF CSELKCESS'S CITIZENS THAT ARE CRYING OUT FOR OUR HELP.

BUT YOU SAID THIS GUY'S HOLED UP UNDER THE CITY, RIGHT? HOW ARE WE SUPPOSED TO GET TO HIM?

ALL RIGHT, IT'S DE-CIDED THEN.

LET'S GO!

IT'S GUARDED BY POWERFUL CHIMERAS, BUT WE SHOULD BE ABLE TO PASS WITH THESE MEMBERS.

THE TUNNEL THAT I TRAVELED THROUGH WITH MAY LED TO THE LAIR OF THIS SO-CALLED FATHER.

REAL-LY?

I KNOW OF ONE EN-TRANCE DOWN THERE.

YES, SOMEONE SHOULD STAY HERE IN CASE MR. FOO COMES BACK.

ALL RIGHT.

DR. MARCOH, YOU SHOULD STAY HERE TOO.

HEINKEL, YOU STAY ON GUARD HERE.

FOR EVERYONE?

I'LL GET HORSES.

NOD NOD NOD

YOKI... YOU STAY HERE TOO.

WHAT IS IT, BIG BROTHER?

AL.

...BE CAREFUL.

WE'RE GONNA GO KICK THE CRAP OUT OF THAT BEARDED GUY WHO LIVES UNDERGROUND.

102

ORDER YOUR BRIGGS TROOPS TO STAND DOWN IMMEDI- ATELY...

...MA- JOR GEN- ERAL ARM- STRONG !!

WOOO WOOO

WOOO

WOOO

WOOO

YES, HE TOLD ME.

ABOUT WHAT'S BEING SACRIFICED AND WHAT HE'S TRYING TO ACHIEVE?

THIS SO- CALLED FATHER TOLD YOU, DIDN'T HE?

DO YOU REALLY THINK YOU CAN GET AWAY WITH THIS?!!

THE SACRI- FICES THAT ACCOM- PANY THIS TRANS- FORMATION CAN'T BE HELPED !!

DON'T YOU SEE? IT'S FOR THE GREATER GOOD!

WE, THE CHOSEN ONES, WILL ASCEND TO EVEN GREATER HEIGHTS, AND THIS COUNTRY OF AMESTRIS WILL CHANGE THE WORLD!

I'D LIKE TO ASK YOU THE SAME QUES- TION.

WHA... ?

YOU BASTARDS ARE HOPELESS.

SWISH

SHF

BAH!

SLIP...

GSHH

SCUM LIKE YOU WHO OBSERVE THE BATTLEFIELD FROM A SAFE LOCATION...

...TALK ABOUT "SACRIFICE" AS IF IT'S SOMETHING SUBLIME. *YOU DON'T EVEN KNOW THE MEANING OF THE WORD!*

OW OW OW!!

I'M NOT AS SOFT AS THE "HERO OF ISHBAL."

WAIT...

BY THE TIME ALL OF THIS IS OVER, I MIGHT BE A HERO. BUT ONE THING'S CERTAIN...

WHO KNOWS?

TUG

WILL YOU TURN TRAITOR, ARMSTRONG?!

BLAM

WHAT'S GOING ON IN—?

!!

FWUMP

WOOO
WOOO
WOOO
WOOO
WOOO
WOOO
WOOO
WOOO
WOOO

107

I SAW THE SMOKE FROM MY HOUSE... DID SOMETHING HAPPEN, SIR?

ISN'T THIS YOUR DAY OFF?

MAJOR ARMSTRONG!

SERGEANT BROSCH!

...

FIRST HE MURDERS 2ND LT. ROSS IN COLD BLOOD, AND NOW HE'S TAKING THE PRESIDENT'S WIFE HOSTAGE?!!

HOW COWARDLY OF HIM!!

HE MUST BE THE DEVIL!!

LET'S SEE... COLONEL MUSTANG AND HIS FORMER SUBORDINATES HAVE TAKEN THE PRESIDENT'S WIFE HOSTAGE AND ARE CURRENTLY ON THE RUN INSIDE THE CITY.

HUH?

WHY WOULD THEY DO THAT?!

MEANWHILE, A GROUP OF ELITE SOLDIERS THOUGHT TO BE NORTHERN TROOPS ARE ATTACKING THE CENTRAL CITY ARMY.

APPARENTLY, THEY'RE MOVING THROUGH THE CITY IN AN ARMORED VEHICLE THAT'S DISGUISED AS AN ICE CREAM TRUCK.

MY OLDER SISTER?!

MAJOR GENERAL ARM-STRONG IS INSIDE THE MILITARY HIGH COMMAND CON-FERENCE ROOM, AND...

MA-JOR!

HMM... THINGS ARE HAPPENING QUICKER THAN I HAD ANTICIPATED.

I NEED TO HURRY AND FIND THE PRINCE.

WHAT COULD GREED BE PLANNING...?

I CAN'T TRACK GREED BY HIS PRESENCE BECAUSE IT'S BEING OVERSHADOWED BY THE MASSIVE PRESENCE THAT'S LURKING BENEATH THE CITY.

I WONDER...

GWOOM

GWOOM GWOOM

THE PRESENCE UNDERGROUND SEEMS TO HAVE GROWN MUCH LARGER THAN IT WAS JUST A DAY AGO...

GWOOM GWOOM

GWOOM

GWOOM GWOOM

110

111

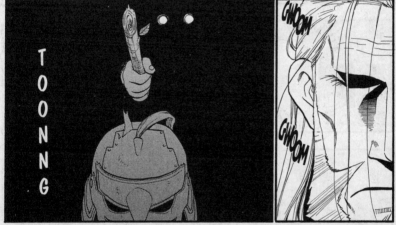

112

THE MILITARY IS USING THIS AREA AS A RALLYING POINT. THERE'S NO WAY WE CAN EVEN GET CLOSE.

IT'S NO USE.

HMM...!!

DAMN IT...

IT WON'T BE EASY TO FORCE OUR WAY THROUGH.

!

AL AND THE COLONEL ONCE SNUCK IN THROUGH THERE TO FIGHT LUST!

LABORATORY NUMBER THREE!!

I KNOW! THERE'S ANOTHER ENTRANCE THAT GOES *UNDERGROUND!*

THREE GUARDS AT THE ENTRANCE...

DASH!

I'M EDWARD ELRIC, THE STATE ALCHEMIST!!

HELP ME, MR. SOLDIER!!

WAIT, NOW'S THE TIME FOR ME TO MAKE USE OF MY TITLE.

KRIK KRAK

HERE I GO.

ALL RIGHT, LET'S DO THIS.

SCAR IS CHASING ME! HELP!!

HUH? WHA? A STATE ALCHEMIST?!

FREEZE!!

THERE'S THE WANTED FUGITIVE!!

HEY!!

WHAT...?

SHOULD WE SPLIT UP INTO TWO GROUPS?

YEAH.

SQUEE
KLANK
KLAK KLAK

KREEAK

I'LL GO THIS WAY. EDWARD AND SCAR GO THAT WAY.

WHAA?!

ALL RIGHT.

BECAUSE DIVIDING THE GROUPS BY THEIR SKILL IN ALCHEMY MAKES THE MOST SENSE.

WHY DO I HAVE TO GO WITH *HIM*?!!

MY ALCHEMY IS *SPECIAL* SO I'LL BE FINE ON MY OWN.

BUT...

THEN IT'S SETTLED. THESE TWO ARE IN THE SAME GROUP.

URK!

PLUS WHEN *THE ENEMY* USED HIS POWER TO BLOCK YOUR ALCHEMY, YOU WERE TOTALLY HELPLESS, BUT SCAR WAS STILL ABLE TO USE HIS, RIGHT?

THE YOUNG LADY FROM XING SEEMS LIKE A GOOD CHOICE.

I COULD USE A *BODY-GUARD.*

DON'T WORRY, WE'LL BE FINE.

WILL YOU REALLY BE ALL RIGHT WITH ONLY TWO OF YOU?

IF ANY OF US RUNS INTO THE ENEMY, LET'S PLAN ON GOING ALL OUT TO DESTROY HIM.

AYE, AYE.

OLD GUYS LIKE ME PREFER BEING WITH YOUNG WOMEN. ♡

GRIT GRIT GRIT

KLAK
KLAK
KLAK
KLAK

C'MON, LET'S GO.

THE OLD LETCH.

GRIT GRIT GRIT

YOU HAVE TO SEARCH FOR THE PRINCE OF XING, RIGHT?

THEN GO.

...

TAT

NOD

HE'S IM-PORTANT TO YOU, ISN'T HE?

BUT...

ER... UH...

DON'T WORRY ABOUT US.

THMP

TMP

LEAP

THANK YOU...

...VERY MUCH.

TUP
TUP
TUP
TUP
TUP TUP
TUP
TUP TUP

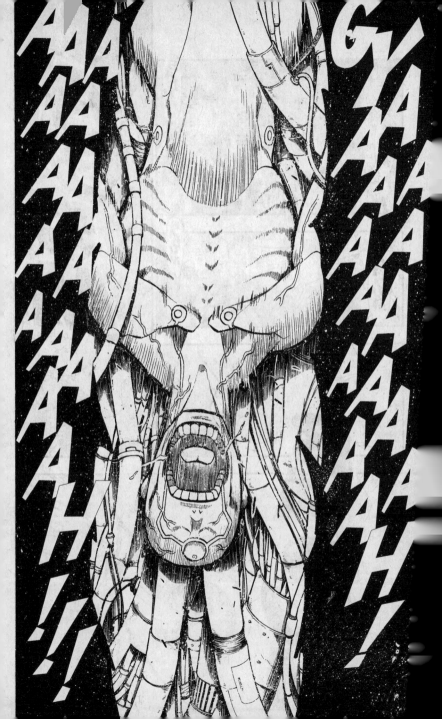

123

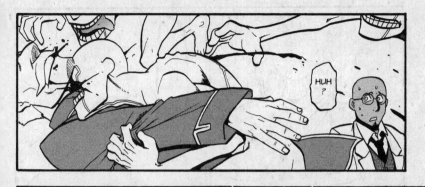

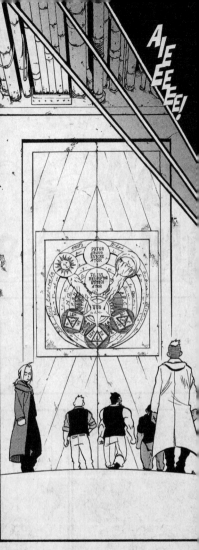

AIEEEE!

I'M GETTING A BAD FEELING.

IT'S A HUGE... DOOR?

WHO'S THIS?

SO THIS IS WHERE HE WAS KILLED...

IT'S BARRY THE CHOPPER...

...WHICH MEANS THERE'S PROBABLY SOMETHING BEHIND THIS THING.

128

I NEVER THOUGHT THAT WAITING AROUND COULD BE SO FRUSTRATING.

I HATE NOT BEING THERE FIGHTING ALONGSIDE THEM.

MUTTER MUTTER

I WONDER IF THOSE GUYS ARE DOING ALL RIGHT?

TONNG
TAK
TONNG
TAK

THAT BANGING SOUND'S BEEN GETTING ON MY NERVES SINCE YESTERDAY!

TAK
TONNG
TONNG
TAK

SELIM'S PLAYING WITH MY HEAD.

TAK
TONNG

TAK
TONNG

TONNG
TONNG

HEY, AL-PHONSE!

WHAT'S THAT SOUND?!

TONNG
TONNG
TONNG

TAK
TAK
TAK

TAK
TONNG
TONNG
TONNG

HUMPH.

HE'S A MONSTER ON THE INSIDE, BUT I GUESS IN THE END HE'S JUST A KID...

HEL-LO.

THANK YOU FOR COMING TO PICK ME UP, KIMBLEE.

HA HA HA.

FOR-GIVE ME.

ZWOO

YOU KNOW, I DO HAVE PLACES TO BE.

I WON'T LET MY GUARD DOWN AGAIN.

FULLMETAL
ALCHEMIST

WUZA WUZA WUZA

WHAT ARE SOLDIERS DOING IN A PLACE LIKE THIS?

ARE THEY HERE TO ISSUE AN EVACUATION ORDER?

WE CAN'T LET THEM FIND OUT THAT YOU'RE DR. MARCOH!!

BUT I CAN'T JUST SIT BY AND WATCH...

WUZA WUZA WUZA WUZA

WE HAVE NO-WHERE ELSE TO GO...

I HOPE NOT.

W... WAIT, DOCTOR!!

OH NO... ALPHONSE IS IN DANGER!

DON'T BE STUPID! IF YOU GET TAKEN HOSTAGE, YOU WON'T BE HELPING ALPHONSE AND THE OTHERS!

RRGH...

LET'S JUST STAY PUT FOR NOW!

OKAY ?!

I HEARD THAT GLUTTONY WAS WITH YOU. WHERE DID HE GO?

ARE YOU BY YOURSELF ?

OH, I ATE HIM.

IS THAT SO?

WE JUST WENT BACK TO BEING ONE, THAT'S ALL.

BOTH OF US WERE BORN FROM THE SAME FATHER.

YOUR ALLY?

?

YOU *ATE* HIM?

HE WAS NO ALLY.

WE'RE ONE AND THE SAME.

TOSS

GGG...

RRR...

GEHOFF...

MR. HEIN-KEL!!

!

TONK

!!

GO... SAVE YOUR- SELF...

DON'T WORRY... ABOUT ME...

SHF
KLANK

AT THIS RATE, WE'LL *BOTH* BE DEAD.

DON'T BE NAIVE.

NO !!

KLANK SHF

KLANK

KLANK

KLANK

KLANK

KLANK

SHRF

SHRF

IF YOU LEAVE ME BEHIND, AT LEAST YOU MIGHT SURVIVE.

I SAID NO!

LEAVE ME BEHIND...

WE'RE UP AGAINST KIMBLEE AND PRIDE.

KOFF

YOU GOTTA FACE REALITY, YOU FOOL...

SRF

KLANK

KLANK

DON'T WORRY ABOUT ANYTHING ELSE—JUST THINK ABOUT SURVIVING !!

AGH!!

KAKLUNK

SN

AP

I'LL HELP YOU ESCAPE NO MATTER WHAT—

DON'T GIVE UP!!

DAMMIT!! WHY WON'T THESE LEGS MOVE?!

SKRICH

WE CAN'T AFFORD TO BE BEATEN YET!!

TONK

TONK

TONK

SHF SHF

JEEZ... YOU BROTHERS...

DON'T GIVE UP!!

KLANK

HANG ON, MR. HEINKEL!!

WHY ARE YOU TWO ALWAYS TRYING TO HELP PEOPLE WHEN YOUR OWN BODIES ARE FALLING APART?

KOFF

SHF SHF

SHRF

THANKS TO HIM, I JUST REMEMBERED SOMETHING THAT MIGHT SHIFT THE ODDS.

KIMBLEE ALWAYS USED TO SAY THAT THE LAST ONE STANDING IS THE WINNER.

THAT'S RIGHT...

THEY WON'T ESCAPE VERY FAR ON THOSE LEGS.

SNIFF

NO.

THOSE TWO ARE STILL INSIDE THE DUST CLOUD.

BIZA

ASHH

?!!

RISE

KRAKLE

KLA NG

WELL, WELL.

HE'S NOT TRYING TO ESCAPE AT ALL!

MOST IMPRESSIVE, ALPHONSE ELRIC!!

IMPRES-SIVE!!

148

SHF..

BAM

WHY—

—YOU !!

RRGH !!

BAM

BAM

OH...

I...

POP

I'M FREEEE!!

GLOMP

EEEEEEEEK!!

152

CURSES! THERE GOES MY ONLY CLUE TO IMMORTALITY!

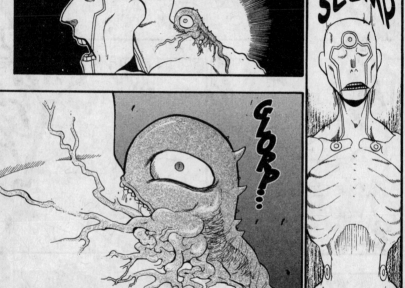

SLUMP

GLORP!...

CHOMP

?!

AAAAAGAAAGU

154

MISHI

MEKI MOGI MUKI

AGH...

MEKI

I'M BAAACK!!

MEKI

MUKI MOGI MISHI

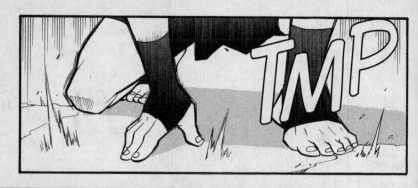

TMP
TMP
TMP
TMP
TMP

WUZA WUZA

WUZA
WUZA WUZA
WUZA

WUZA

TMP
TMP
TMP
TMP

TMP

TMP

RR... GH...

POK

ORDER THEM TO WITHDRAW ALL CENTRAL CITY TROOPS THAT ARE FIGHTING MUSTANG AND THE BRIGGS SOLDIERS.

IF YOU'RE GOING TO SHOOT, SHOOT.

CHAK

CHAK

YEOOW!!

I DON'T THINK YOUR SUBORDINATES ARE TAKING ME SERIOUSLY.

SHUNK

...

WELL ?

IF YOU DON'T WITHDRAW YOUR MEN, THE BRIGGS TROOPS WON'T HESITATE TO KEEP FIGHTING.

...RRGH!

CLOSE THE NORTHERN, SOUTHERN, EASTERN AND WESTERN GATES OF THE CENTRAL CITY HEAD-QUARTERS!! CLOSE ALL THE GATES!!

HMM..

YOU'RE ROTTEN, BUT IT SEEMS YOU'RE NOT TOTALLY SPINELESS AFTER ALL.

DON'T LET A SINGLE ONE OF THE BRIGGS TROOPS NOR MUSTANG'S MEN INSIDE!!

!

OH !!

I'LL SQUASH ALL OF YOU BRIGGS MONKEYS! I'LL—

YOU ARROGANT WENCH!!

HUH
?

TWITCH

KRACK

161

162

THERE'S NO END TO THEM!!

UHH!

WHOA!

GLARE

KRACK

?!

SHHK
RG!
RIP
DANGLE
GE!

SNAP

SWIP...

SPUTTER
SPUTTER

OOAH...

OWAH!
UWAAGH!

AND WHY WON'T THEY DIE?!

WHAT THE HECK ARE THESE CREEPY THINGS?!!

THOK

SMAK

THEY'VE ATTACHED **PEOPLE'S SOULS** ONTO THESE DOLLS!!

THESE THINGS...

BAM

YOU MEAN, LIKE AL-PHONSE?!

THEN HOW DO WE KILL THEM?!!

OUCH!

CHOMP

166

THWACK

MY THICK NECK SAVED ME...

!

PEH!

STOP!!

SMEK SMEK

CLAP

I'M ON IT!!

ED!

167

BZASH

...THERE'S NOWHERE LEFT FOR THEM TO RUN!

AND NOW...

MEKI

OMPH!

SORRY. I BLOCKED OFF THE EXIT.

DON'T WORRY ABOUT IT.

IF YOU HADN'T DONE IT, WE WOULD'VE DESTROYED THE EXIT OUR-SELVES.

FOR SOME REASON IT MAKES ME MAD WHEN YOU'RE AGREEING WITH US...

EXACTLY. WE CAN'T RISK LETTING THESE GET OUTSIDE.

GUOOOOO...

DROOL DROOL DROOL

...

HOW COULD THEY MAKE SUCH THINGS?

WAAH WAAH

IT HURTS.

I'M HUNGRY.

MA-MA...

AAAAH!

OHHH...

LURCH

LURCH

LURCH

LURCH

IN ANY CASE, WE NEED TO GET PAST THEM IF WE'RE GONNA KICK THE CRAP OUT OF THE BEARDED GUY.

IT AIN'T GONNA BE EASY!!

I WAS SURE YOU'D BRING THE BROTHERS TOO.

YOU CAME ALONE?

...DWARF IN THE FLASK?

RIGHT...

HUP

I DON'T NEED THAT MANY PEOPLE JUST TO SCOLD ONE LITTLE TROUBLE-MAKING BRAT LIKE YOU.

SLAVE TWENTY-THREE, YOU ONCE GAVE ME A PART OF YOURSELF.

SNAP

THIS TIME, YOU WILL BECOME A PART OF ME.

Fullmetal Alchemist 22 End

FULLMETAL
ALCHEMIST

EXTRAS

From Chapter 91

DON'T GIVE UP!!

DRAG DRAG

HANG ON, MR. HEINKEL!!

WHY DO YOU INSIST ON HELPING ME WHEN YOUR OWN BODY IS FALLING APART?

OH, REALLY?

BE-CAUSE YOU'RE A CAT!!!

↑ Homo Sapiens Felinus

FORTUNES

ROACH MOTEL

FULLMETAL SCIENCE KIDS!

NO WAY.

AL GOT MORE THAN I DID!!

HEY!! DON'T SPILL IT...

TODAY YOU CAN HAVE SOME JUICE FOR SNACK TIME.

BIG BROTHER, YOU'RE SHORT, THAT'S WHY YOUR LINE OF SIGHT IS WRONG!!

YOUR LINE OF SIGHT HAS TO BE EQUAL WITH THE SURFACE OF THE WATER!!

...SEE?? AL, YOU GOT 1.3 MILLILITERS MORE THAN ME!!

YES WAY!! GO GET THE GRADUATED CYLINDERS FROM HOHENHEIM'S ROOM!!

I AM LOOKING AT IT THE RIGHT WAY, STUPID!!

THAT'S IMPOSSIBLE!! THE RATE OF CUBICAL EXPANSION IS 0.00021 TO EACH ONE DEGREE CELSIUS INCREASE!!

IT COULDN'T HAVE INCREASED THAT MUCH!!

IT...IT'S CUBICAL EXPANSION!! MY SEAT IS IN THE SUNLIGHT, SO THE TEMPERATURE OF THE JUICE INCREASED AND CAUSED THE VOLUME TO INCREASE TOO!!

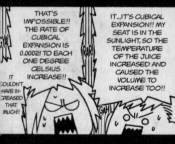

SMART KIDS CAN BE SUCH A PAIN...

THEN, BIG BROTHER, YOUR JUICE MUST'VE EVAPORATED AND...

NU-UH, IT'S...

NO WAY, IT'S...

THE DANGERS OF OVEREATING

GOBBLE!

WAAH!

MUNCH MUNCH

MUNCH

HEH HEH HEH... I'VE ACQUIRED GLUTTONY'S ABILITIES.

CHUBBA!

NOW I HAVE THE ADVANTAGE...

THINK YOU'VE MADE A MISTAKE...

CAMPAIGN PROMISES

THE MAJOR GENERAL COMES FROM A DISTINGUISHED FAMILY, SO SHE MUST HAVE A LOT OF CONNECTIONS.

DO YOU THINK COLONEL MUSTANG STANDS A CHANCE AGAINST HER?

PSP

WSP

PSP

REALLY?

WSP

PSP

I HEAR THAT MAJOR GENERAL ARMSTRONG IS AIMING TO BECOME PRESIDENT TOO.

OKAY!! WELL IN THAT CASE, I'M SURE EVERYONE WILL VOTE FOR THE COLONEL!

HA HA!

AFTER ALL, THE COLONEL'S PROMISED TO CHANGE THE FEMALE MILITARY UNIFORMS TO MINISKIRTS IF HE'S ELECTED!!

WA HA HA!

DON'T WORRY!

Refer to volume 3 extras.

Major General Armstrong's Approval Rating

Colonel Mustang's Approval Rating

VERY WELL, THEN. I APPROVE!

A MINISKIRT GOVERNMENT? WILL THAT INCREASE WORK EFFICIENCY?

CONSENT!

ZOOOOM!

rmstrong's

's Approval Rating

THE ROACH'S REVENGE

HA HA HA HA! THAT TICKLES, DEN.

HI, DID ANYTHING SPECIAL HAPPEN WHILE I WAS GONE?

WE'RE HOME!

OH, WELCOME HOME, ED.

NO... NOT REALLY...

LICK LICK LICK

CRUNCH

FULLMETAL ALCHEMIST 22

SPECIAL THANKS to:

Jun Tohko

Noriko Tsubota

Kori Sakano

Masashi Mizutani

Haruhi Nakamura

Manatsu Sakura

Coupon

Kazufumi Kaneko

Kei Takanamazu

My Editor, Yuichi Shimomura

AND YOU!!

FULLMETAL ALCHEMIST

The paper that I've been using for my color illustrations all this time is no longer being made. This was the biggest shock of the year!

—Hiromu Arakawa, 2009

FULLMETAL
ALCHEMIST

■ アルフォンス・エルリック

Alphonse Elric

■ エドワード・エルリック

Edward Elric

■ アレックス・ルイ・アームストロング

Alex Louis Armstrong

■ ロイ・マスタング

Roy Mustang

OUTLINE
FULLMETAL ALCHEMIST

Using a forbidden alchemical ritual, the Elric brothers attempted to bring their dead mother back to life. But the ritual went wrong, consuming Edward Elric's leg and Alphonse Elric's entire body. At the cost of his arm, Edward was able to graft his brother's soul into a suit of armor. Equipped with mechanical "auto-mail" to replace his missing limbs, Edward becomes a state alchemist in hopes of finding a way to restore their bodies. Their search embroils them in a deadly conspiracy that threatens to take the innocence, if not the lives, of everyone involved.

As the "Day of Reckoning" approaches, Central City has become a war zone! On one side, the Homunculi and the military leaders who have sold out their country for power; on the other, a ragtag alliance of rebel soldiers loyal to Major General Armstrong and Roy Mustang, Ishbalan refugees and, of course, the Elric family and their allies. As things heat up on the streets, Ed, Hohenheim and Scar descend into "Father's" underground complex where they stumble upon the military's top-secret army of artificial humans. Meanwhile, on the outskirts of the capital, Al confronts the Homunculus Pride and the murderous alchemist Kimblee.

鋼の錬金術師
FULLMETAL ALCHEMIST

CHARACTERS
FULLMETAL ALCHEMIST

■ セリム・ブラッドレイ（プライド）

Selim Bradley (Pride)

■ スカー

Scar

■ オリヴィエ・ミラ・アームストロング

Olivier Mira Armstrong

■ キング・ブラッドレイ

King Bradley

■ スロウス

Sloth

■ ゾルフ・J・キンブリー

Solf J. Kimblee

CONTENTS

THE PHILOS-OPHER'S STONE!!

IT'S TRUE THAT WE MIGHT BE ABLE TO WIN IF I USE THIS...

YOUR BROTHER TOLD ME THAT HE REFUSES TO USE THIS TO GET YOUR ORIGINAL BODIES BACK.

YEAH, I KNOW.

THIS IS MADE FROM HUMAN LIVES.

...BUT ...!!

KOFF

YOU STILL CONSIDER THOSE SACRIFICED SOULS TO BE HUMAN EVEN THOUGH THEY'VE BEEN TURNED INTO A TINY PEBBLE LIKE THIS. THAT'S WHY I'M ASKING YOU TO USE IT.

THEN INSTEAD OF USING IT FOR YOURSELVES, USE IT TO PROTECT THIS WORLD.

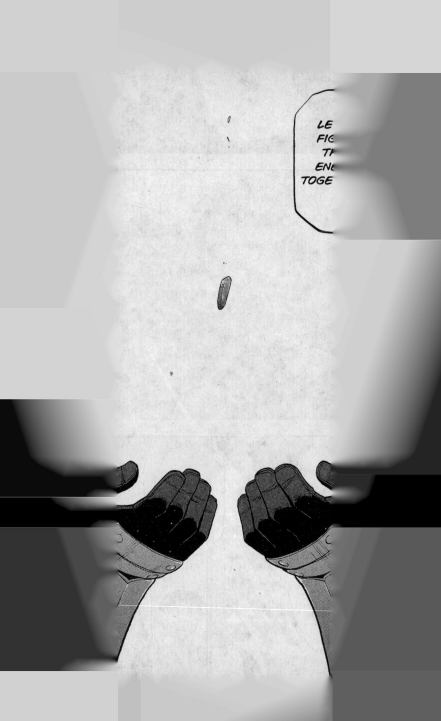

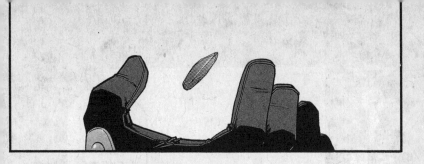

WHAP

WHAM

WHERE DID YOU GET THAT?

A PHILOSOPHER'S STONE!!

BWOOO...

BUT THERE'S ONE THING I DON'T UNDERSTAND.

THE POWER OF THE PHILOSOPHER'S STONE IS TRULY AMAZING.

SHUP

I'VE USED IT MYSELF, SO I FULLY UNDERSTAND WHAT IT CAN DO.

STAGGER

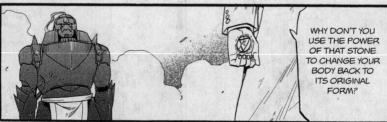

WHY DON'T YOU USE THE POWER OF THAT STONE TO CHANGE YOUR BODY BACK TO ITS ORIGINAL FORM?

THEN, WOULDN'T THAT BE THE END OF YOUR JOURNEY?

YOU COULD FIND YOUR BROTHER, AND THE TWO OF YOU WOULD BE BACK TO NORMAL, JUST LIKE THAT.

WITH THE STONE IN YOUR POSSESSION, YOU COULD EASILY ESCAPE FROM US.

ABOUT THAT.

YOU KNOW HOW THINGS WORK. IN ORDER TO GET SOMETHING, ANOTHER THING MUST BE SACRIFICED.

BUT YOU COULD ACHIEVE YOUR ULTIMATE GOAL.

WE WOULDN'T BE ABLE TO SAVE ANYONE BY DOING THAT.

...OR WE GIVE UP OUR GOAL SO WE CAN SAVE EVERYONE. THOSE AREN'T THE ONLY TWO AVAILABLE CHOICES, YOU KNOW.

EITHER WE GET OUR ORIGINAL BODIES BACK BUT CAN'T SAVE ANYONE...

WHY ARE THERE ONLY **TWO** CHOICES?

WHO'S TO SAY WE CAN'T GET OUR FLESH AND BLOOD BODIES BACK *AND* SAVE EVERYONE?

HUMANITY'S ADVANCEMENT IS FOUNDED ON LOOKING FOR NEW POSSIBILITIES INSTEAD OF BEING BOUND BY GENERAL PRINCIPLES.

WHAT ABOUT THE LAW OF EQUIV-ALENT EX-CHANGE?

YOU WON'T BE ABLE TO REGAIN YOUR ORIGINAL BODIES *NOR* SAVE ANYONE. YOU'D DO WELL TO BEWARE OF THAT OUTCOME.

IN OTHER WORDS, IF YOU'RE SUCCESSFUL, THEN THE LAWS OF NATURE WILL CHANGE TO FIT THE NEW REALITY.

OH, I SEE.

PAT

THEN HERE'S ANOTHER POSSI-BILITY.

SO BULLETS HAVE NO EFFECT.

TROMP

HIGH COMMAND HAS CHARGED YOU WITH TREASON AND ORDERED YOU SHOT ON SIGHT!!

YOU CAN'T ESCAPE, MAJOR GENERAL ARMSTRONG!

TROMP TROMP

READY! AIM!

FI--

RRG ?!

KRAK

KER-

PLUK

WHAT A FOOL, KEEPING YOUR MEN BUNCHED UP IN A SITUATION LIKE THIS!

KA BOOM

FWIP

?

KOFF GACH KOFF

KOFF

!! CLOMP

I HOPE THAT AT LEAST WOUNDS THE BRUTE...

MOWU

MOWU

208

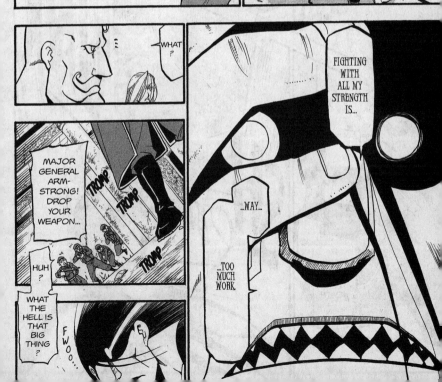

THWOMP

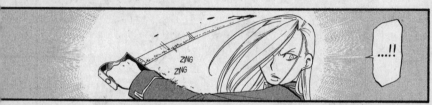

ZING
ZING

.....!!

THIS THING... ALL THIS TIME IT WAS JUST BEING LAZY!

SUCH SPEED...

I'M FINE. IT JUST GRAZED MY ARM.

SIS!!

IT WAS A BLUR!

WERE YOU ABLE TO FOLLOW THAT?

IT'S A BIT UNFAIR, ISN'T IT?

SKIG

BEING ABLE TO MOVE AT THAT SPEED DESPITE ITS WEIGHT...

VIP

YUP.

I'M...

...THE FASTEST HOMUNCULUS.

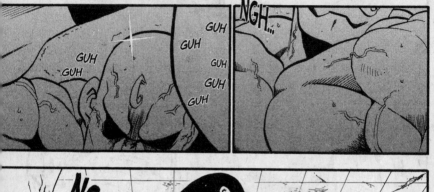

I DOUBT HE WOULD RUN AWAY.

GRIT...

BOOM

BOOM

BOOM

TOSS

TING

K A N G

BOOM

BOOM

BOOM

BOOM

AAAH !!!

THERE YOU ARE!!

BAM

BOOF

HUP!

SLAP

WHOOM!

SNIF

SNIF

ANOTHER SMOKE SCREEN? HOW PREDICTABLE...

ZWOO

ZWOO

IT'S NO USE.

228

229

SHUNK

SHUNK

NOW I'LL SHOW YOU HOW TENACIOUS HUMANS CAN BE.

WHO SAID I WAS ALONE ?!

YOU MAY HAVE A PHILOSOPHER'S STONE, BUT THERE'S NO WAY THAT YOU CAN DEFEAT US ON YOUR OWN!

WHERE DID HE PUT THE STONE...?

?!

THIS DUST CLOUD WASN'T JUST MEANT TO GIVE ALPHONSE COVER...

IT CAN'T BE...!!

HE WAS USING IT TO CONCEAL THE ACTIONS OF HIS ALLIES DOWNWIND, WHERE MY SENSE OF SMELL CAN'T REACH!!

KIMBLEE!! THEY'RE COMING FROM DOWN--

233

FLINCH

. . .

. . .

BASED ON HIS PERSONALITY, I THOUGHT HE WOULD ATTACK WITHOUT REGARD FOR KIMBLEE'S LIFE.

WHAT THE...?

IS IT HOLDING BACK BECAUSE I'M USING KIMBLEE AS A SHIELD?

BUT YOUR KIND CAN NEVER WIN...

JUST AS YOU SAID, HUMANS ARE A TENACIOUS LOT.

I SEE.

...NOT WHILE FATHER IS IN CENTRAL CITY.

SKREE

!!

TWIK

NOT THAT THAT'S YOUR PROBLEM. YOU'LL NEVER LEAVE THIS PLACE ALIVE.

VRMM

236

237

238

BONK
OUCH
KATH

I HAVE NO INTENTION OF FIGHTING THAT MONSTER FACE-TO-FACE!!

KLATA
RATTA
THUNK
KLATA

WE'LL HOOK BACK UP WITH ED AND THE OTHERS SO WE CAN DESTROY THIS SO-CALLED FATHER BEFORE THAT THING CATCHES UP TO US!!

GO TO CENTRAL CITY!!

VROOOOOOOSH

VROOOM
CRUNCH
SNAP

CRUNCH

HUMANS LIKE THEM, BLINDED BY THEIR SENSE OF DUTY, ARE SO EASY TO TRICK.

CRUNCH

CRUNCH

HUFF... WEEZ...

WEEZ... WEEZ...

YOU'RE STILL ALIVE.

OH GOOD.

IT APPEARS YOU HUMANS AREN'T AT THE TOP OF THE FOOD CHAIN AFTER ALL!

GRIN

HE FOLLOWED THE LAW OF THE JUNGLE, SURVIVAL OF THE FITTEST, AND WENT STRAIGHT FOR YOUR THROAT.

THAT OLD FRIEND OF YOURS IS TRULY THE KING OF BEASTS.

YOUR SUIT'S NEW COLOR LOOKS GOOD ON YOU, KIMBLEE.

IT MUST BE UTTERLY HUMILIATING TO PERISH IN A PLACE LIKE THIS.

...YOU WANTED TO SEE WHAT PATH THE WORLD WOULD CHOOSE, DIDN'T YOU?

YOU SAID THAT...

WEEZ... GAGH.

GUCK.

KOFF

BUT DON'T WORRY.

ZWU...

ALCHEMY SURE COMES IN HANDY.

CENTRAL MEAT

DOESN'T IT?

USING ALCHEMY, CHANGING THE EXTERIOR OF THE TRUCK IS EASY.

ISN'T THAT KINDA CONSPICUOUS?

FOR REAL?

APPARENTLY THE RENEGADES ARE DRIVING AN ICE CREAM TRUCK.

VROOM

SO... IT'S NO GOOD OVER HERE EITHER.

JUST AS WE FEARED, SIR.

VROOM

ALL THE GATES IN EVERY DIRECTION HAVE BEEN CLOSED OFF.

246

WHAT
HAP-
PENED
...?

UGH...

RRGH...

TROMP

TROMP

TROMP

SPLURT

DRIP DRIP
DRIP
DRIP

ALEX
!!

WE KNOW IT'LL COME CHARGING IN, SO ALL WE HAVE TO DO IS LIE IN WAIT!

249

WHAT?!

THAT'S TER-RIBLE!!

OH YEAH, THEY'VE ISSUED AN ORDER TO SHOOT ME ON SIGHT.

DON'T WORRY ABOUT IT!

I'VE DECIDED TO GIVE THE FAMILY MANSION TO MUSTANG IF I DIE!

I'M GOING TO BE THE HEAD OF THE FAMILY, SO YOU NEED TO SIGN THE PROPER DOCUMENTS BEFORE YOU DIE!

GASHUNK

RRGH...

TOO MUCH. ...WORK.

IS THAT HOW YOU SPEAK TO THE PERSON WHO JUST SAVED YOUR LIFE?!

GYAA GYAA

SQABBLE SQABBLE

BETTER AN IDIOT OUTSIDER THAN A TOTAL INCOMPETENT LIKE YOU!

W-WHAT THE HECK IS THAT?

RR

GG

NO IDEA...

I KEEP SHOOTING THEM, BUT THEY WON'T DIE!!

RAT-TA-TAT

TAT-TA-TAT-TA-TAT

W-WHAT THE HELL ARE THOSE THINGS?!!

CRUNK

THEY'RE PROBABLY RELATED TO *THIS* THING.

THEY'RE BEING CONTROLLED BY THE SAME PEOPLE WHO ARE GIVING YOU ORDERS.

YOU IDIOT!! DON'T MISTAKE MY POWERFUL TROOPS WITH THOSE PALE, SCRAWNY RUNTS!!

GYAAAH!

ARE THEY BRIGGS TROOPS?!

AIEEE!

BLAM

WAAAH!

SEEMS LIKE THEY DON'T CARE WHETHER YOU KNEW ABOUT IT OR NOT, DOESN'T IT?

WE HAVEN'T BEEN INFORMED OF ANY SUCH THING!!

HNK SHNK SHNK

URGH...

FSHHH

WHAT WILL YOU DO?

IF YOU WANT, MY BROTHER AND I CAN TAKE THOSE MONSTERS ON.

TAT-TAT

HELP! HELP!

BLAM

ER...

FLINCH

WUMP

SNAP

KRIK

GLUK

KRAK

KRE EEEE...

WELL? WHAT ARE YOU GOING TO DO?!

TMP

TRMBL TRMBL

WILL YOU KILL US NOW, ONLY TO BE SLAUGHTERED BY THAT MONSTER?!

MAKE YOUR OWN CHOICE !!

OR WILL YOU COOPERATE WITH US TO BRING IT DOWN?!

IT'S NO USE! THESE LIVING DOLL SOLDIERS ARE FUELED BY PHILOSOPHER'S STONES!

GRAAH

UH...

EEEEEEK?!

GH!

SNAP

IT'LL TAKE MORE THAN THAT TO KILL THEM!

GLUNCH

VOOM

ARE YOU CALLING ME INFERIOR TO THOSE PATHETIC TOYS?!

DON'T MAKE ME LAUGH!!

IF THESE DOLLS HAVE HAD A PHILOSOPHER'S STONE INSERTED INTO THEM...

OOOOOOOGH

...I SHOULD BE ABLE TO FIND A LARGE STONE IF I CAN GET TO WHERE THEY CAME FROM!

HII--

IT MAKES YOUR POWERS USE-LESS!

I THOUGHT YOU DIDN'T LIKE WATER, SIR.

I WISH I COULD SEE SUCH PURE EMOTION ON YOUR FACE AGAIN.

I CAN STILL PICTURE YOU CRYING.

THIS PLACE REALLY BRINGS BACK MEMORIES, LIEUTEN-ANT.

HURRY UP AND FIGHT!!

WE'LL TALK LATER!

ER... SCAR!

THOCK

WHAM

WE NEED TO KILL THESE WHITE THINGS, RIGHT?

CHAK

UNDER-STOOD.

DON'T GIVE ME ANY ORDERS.

IRK

263

NOT AGAIN?!

IT TAKES MORE THAN GUNS TO KILL THESE THINGS!!

THAT'S USELESS!

WHAM

IGNORED?!

DRAG

DRAG

I SEE. SO THAT'S WHY YOU'RE ATTACKING THEIR LEGS.

THERE'VE BEEN A LOT OF THOSE RECENTLY...

FOO

STOP GRAND-STAND-ING...

...AND HELP US OUT!!

FSHH FSHH FSHH FSHH FSHH

IF YOU'RE HAVING TROUBLE WITH THESE THINGS, YOU'VE STILL GOT A LONG WAY TO GO.

LUNGE

WHY, YOU... STOP MOVING!!

WHAM BAM WHAM

COME BACK HERE, YOU LITTLE BRAT!!

HUP TUPTUPTUPTUPTUP

ENVY!!

HEY... THAT'S--!

HUH? YOU GUYS...

KOFF KOFF

AW MAN, YOU REALLY DID A NUMBER ON THESE GUYS, DIDN'T YOU?

GI!

GI! GI!

SKICH SKICH

OH, EVEN THOSE DAMNED CHIMERA THAT WERE SO NICE TO ME UP NORTH ARE HERE TOO.

THE FULLMETAL ALCHEMIST, THE FLAME ALCHEMIST AND SCAR...

BUT... BUT...

FOOLISH GIRL! WHY DIDN'T YOU GO BACK TO YOUR COUNTRY?!

MR. SCAR! AND MR. EDWARD!

WHO SHOULD I TAKE CARE OF FIRST?

WELL THEN...

268

THIS IS **ENVY**?

IF I REMEMBER RIGHT, IT'S THE SHAPE-SHIFTING HOMUNCULUS.

SO YOU'VE HEARD OF ME?

NICE TO MEET YOU, COLONEL MUSTANG.

ARE YOU REALLY ALL RIGHT WITH HIM, SCAR?

OH, BUT...

HE'S ONE OF THE STATE ALCHEMISTS THAT FOUGHT IN ISHBAL, ISN'T HE?

...

THAT'S RIGHT.

269

THEN AGAIN, I CAN'T LET THE COLONEL DIE JUST YET! HA HA HA!!

I LOVE WATCHING YOU INSECTS FIGHT AMONGST YOURSELVES!

CAN'T YOU GUYS MUSTER UP A LITTLE GRUDGE MATCH?!

YOU'RE ALLIES NOW?!

HOW BOR-ING!

WE HAVE NO TIME TO GO ALONG WITH YOUR PATHETIC GAMES.

YOU'RE RIGHT! I DO ENJOY WATCHING FOOLS BEING MANIPULATED LIKE PUPPETS!

HEY!!

DON'T YOU HUMANS ALSO LOVE WATCHING FOOLS SUFFER AND DANCE ABOUT LIKE PUPPETS?

ISN'T THAT WHY YOU'RE ALWAYS AT WAR?

PATHETIC? OKAY THEN, LET ME ASK YOU A QUESTION!

IRK

I'VE ANSWERED YOUR QUESTION.

NOW ANSWER MINE.

ESPECIALLY WHEN THOSE FOOLS BEING MANIPULATED ARE HOMUNCULI!

WHO KILLED MAES HUGHES?

IT WASN'T HER.

NO.

...THE ONE YOU BURNED TO DEATH.

IT WAS MARIA ROSS...

...IDIOT.

FOR THE LOVE OF GOD, SHUT UP...

AND? WHAT DID YOU TELL HER PARENTS? DID YOU APOLOGIZE WITH TEARS IN YOUR EYES? OR DID YOU STAY QUIET ABOUT IT BECAUSE YOU WERE AFRAID OF THEIR ANGER?

NICE GOING! HOW CRUEL!

HAH!

SO YOU INCINERATED AN INNOCENT WOMAN!

JUST HURRY UP AND GIVE ME THE FACTS, YOU FOOL.

I'M GETTING TIRED OF ASKING YOU HOMUNCULI THIS QUESTION.'

WHO KILLED HUGHES?

HA HA HA!

HEH HEH HEH HEH.

HEH HEH.

HEH...

!

HEH HEH HEH

CONGRAT-ULATIONS, COLONEL MUSTANG.

G/K

I SEVERELY DOUBT THAT HUGHES COULD'VE BEEN KILLED BY A FOOL LIKE YOU.

YOU'VE FINALLY FOUND YOUR KILLER.

WHAT A GREAT EXPRESSION!!

HAH HA HA!! I WISH YOU COULD SEE YOUR FACE RIGHT NOW!!

PRICELESS!! HA HA HA HA HA HA!!

THE LOOK OF DESPAIR AS HE THOUGHT HE WAS BEING SHOT TO DEATH BY HIS OWN BELOVED WIFE--

TALK ABOUT CRAZY EXPRESSIONS...

KILLING HUGHES WAS GREAT FUN!!

NOW THAT I KNOW THAT AS A FACT...

YOU KILLED HUGHES.

THAT'S SETTLED.

FLINCH

EEP

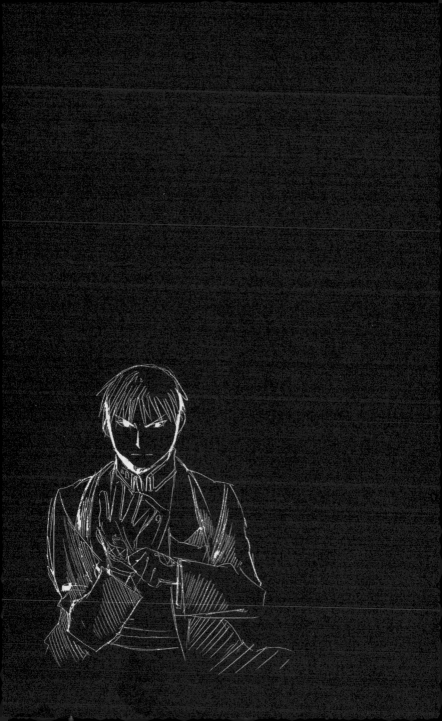

Chapter 94
The Flames of Vengeance

FULLMETAL
ALCHEMIST

THEY POINTED THEIR GUNS AT YOU AND THREATENED TO SHOOT?

YES.

YES.

THE CENTRAL CITY MILITARY TRIED TO KILL ME.

THEY SAID, "KILL HER ALONG WITH MUSTANG'S MEN."

SO SOMEONE HERE IN THE CAPITAL HAS SEIZED THIS OPPORTUNITY TO STAGE A COUP IN THE PRESIDENT'S ABSENCE?

YES.

PRESIDENT BRADLEY HAS GONE TO INSPECT THE EASTERN REGION AND IS PRESENTLY NOT IN CENTRAL CITY, IS THAT TRUE?

RADIO CAPITAL

IS THAT TRUE?

MAYBE IT'S A HOAX?

ALL THE GATES TO CENTRAL COMMAND HAVE BEEN CLOSED, AND I CAN'T GET IN TOUCH WITH ANYONE ON THE INSIDE.

THERE'S NO WAY TO KNOW FOR SURE.

HOW AWFUL.

CHATTER

SOMEONE, PLEASE...

POOR LADY...

I HAVEN'T BEEN ABLE TO GET IN TOUCH WITH MY SON!!

CHATTER

CHATTER

CHATTER

PLEASE... OH... PLEASE

SELIM...!!

I WONDER IF SELIM IS ALL RIGHT.

CHATTER

CAN SOMEBODY OTHER THAN BRADLEY REALLY RUN THIS COUNTRY?

WE'RE ALL GLAD THAT YOU'RE ALIVE AT LEAST.

WHO STAGED THE COUP?

I'M SURE YOUR SON IS FINE, FIRST LADY BRADLEY.

IF... COLONEL MUSTANG HADN'T SAVED ME, WHO KNOWS WHAT WOULD'VE HAPPENED...

NOPE.

WHSP

NO ONE'S TOLD THE PRESIDENT'S WIFE THAT SELIM IS A HOMUNCULUS?

AND NO ONE TOLD HER THAT THE PRESIDENT'S MISSING EITHER.

FWP FWP

PST WHSP

WHSP PST

THE PRESIDENT HIMSELF IS CURRENTLY MISSING.

...BUT A FEW HOURS AGO, SOMEONE BOMBED THE TRAIN THE PRESIDENT WAS RIDING IN.

THE FIRST LADY HASN'T HEARD ABOUT IT YET...

NOW WE KNOW WHAT.

FOR SOME TIME NOW, COLONEL MUSTANG HAS BEEN SUSPICIOUS OF CERTAIN BACKROOM MEETINGS AT HIGH COMMAND. HE'S BEEN CONVINCED THAT SOME OF THE MEMBERS HAVE BEEN PLOTTING SOMETHING.

ARE YOU ALL RIGHT?!!

KLACK

FIRST LADY BRADLEY!!

A FACTION IN HIGH COMMAND IS TRYING TO DEPOSE THE PRESIDENT!!

AAAAH, I'M SORRY!! DON'T SHOOT!!

HEY... WHAT THE...?!

KLAK

TSHH

TSHH

YEAH!!!

THE MEDIA WILL NEVER CAVE TO POLITICAL POWER!!

YOU'D HAVE TO BE AN IDIOT TO STOP A SCOOP LIKE THIS!

ON AIR

ALL RIGHT, DON'T STOP THE BROADCAST!!

PERFECT!

HOW WAS THAT?!

...AND FOR THE SAKE OF JUSTICE, WE ARE PREPARED TO GIVE OUR LIVES TO STOP THESE EVIL MEN FROM CORRUPTING OUR GREAT NATION.

...MEAGER AS OUR EFFORTS MIGHT BE, HAVE TAKEN IT UPON OURSELVES TO CARRY OUT THE WILL OF THE PRESIDENT...

W... WHAT?!

MURMUR

MURMUR

IS BRADLEY DEAD?!

COLONEL MUSTANG AND WE WHO SUPPORT HIM...

MURMUR

CHATTER

CHATTER

286

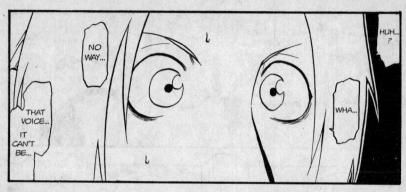

NO WAY...

THAT VOICE... IT CAN'T BE...

HUH...?

WHA...

HOPEFULLY, THE PEOPLE TAKE THE BAIT.

HEE HEE HEE

BUT HOW BOLD OF YOU TO USE THE WORD "JUSTICE."

WITH BRADLEY GONE, WE'RE FREE TO TAKE ADVANTAGE OF THE POWER THAT'S ATTACHED TO HIS NAME.

HA HA HA HA!

HA HA HA

YUP. WHOEVER SAYS IT FIRST WINS.

IT HAS A NICE RING TO IT.

EVERYONE LOVES THAT WORD, DON'T THEY?

I CAN'T BELIEVE YOU USED SUCH A VAGUE, FRIVOLOUS WORD LIKE "JUSTICE."

THE FIRST LADY WAS ALMOST MURDERED!

CHATTER CHATTER CHATTER

WHAT THE HECK IS GOING ON?

I'LL USE WHATEVER WORD I NEED TO.

WE JUST ARRIVED FROM THE EAST AND CAN TELL YOU IT'S A FACT THAT THE PRESIDENT'S TRAIN WAS BLOWN UP.

MUS-TANG'S MEN SPEAK THE TRUTH.

IF RADIO CAPITAL IS ATTACKED AND THE PRESIDENT'S WIFE DIES, WE'LL KNOW FOR SURE THAT THE HIGH COMMAND IS GUILTY.

WHAT'S GONNA HAPPEN TO THE PRESI-DENT AND HIS FAMILY?

WHAT? SO IT REALLY IS A COUP?

THE LEADER OF THEIR COUNTRY IS MISSING, AND YET THEY HAVEN'T TOLD THE PEOPLE?

SO THE PEOPLE OF CENTRAL CITY STILL HAVEN'T HEARD ABOUT THIS?

CHATTER CHATTER CHATTER CHATTER CHATTER CHATTER

WHAT'S TAKING THE URBAN COM-MANDO SQUAD SO LONG?!

WUUU WUUU WUUU

I HOPE HE HASN'T BEEN KILLED...

HE MUST'VE BEEN TAKEN HOS-TAGE...

WHAT ABOUT SELIM?

GAB GAB GAB GAB GAB GAB GAB

SURELY THEY CAN'T POSE A THREAT!

APPARENTLY, THE ENEMY IS BETTER ARMED THAN WE ANTICIPATED. THE COMMANDOS ARE ON THE DEFENSIVE...

288

SIR, IT'S A MESSAGE FROM THE COMMANDO SQUAD!!

IT'S NOT AS IF THEY HAVE A TANK!

?!

THOSE BRIGGS GUYS, THEY EVEN BROUGHT A-- GAAGH!!

GIVE ME A FULL REPORT SPEAK!!

IT TOOK YOU LONG ENOUGH!!

THEY SOUND PANICKED...

GRAB

HM?

...HUH?

EVEN HAD WHAT?!!

HEY!!

KRUNK KRUNK

KRUNK KRUNK

289

THIS PREY IS MINE.

I'LL HANDLE THIS.

FULL-METAL...

SCAR...

WE'LL JUST BE ON OUR WAY THEN...

GREAT!

...

AAAH!!!

GWOOM

BZZT

I STILL NEED TO REPAY YOU FOR WHAT YOU DID TO ME UP NORTH...

WHO SAID YOU COULD LEAVE?!

GLURK GLURK

FOOM

CAN YOU REALLY AFFORD TO BE TALKING TO THEM WHEN YOU'VE GOT **ME** TO DEAL WITH?

CRACKLE

GEGH!

SHOOF

THAT MUST BE WHY IT BURNS ...ENVY. SO WELL...

JUDGING BY HOW MUCH YOU RUN YOUR MOUTH OFF, I'M GUESSING YOU HAVE A RATHER *FAT* TONGUE.

LIEU-TEN-ANT...

ARE YOU SURE THE TWO OF YOU CAN HANDLE THIS?

HAH

GAH

293

WE'LL MANAGE SOME-HOW.

IF WE CAN'T... THEN...

THE COLO-NEL WILL BE FINE.

YOU SAW HOW MUCH FIRE-POWER HE HAS, RIGHT?

THERE'S NO WAY HE'LL LOSE TO THAT HOMUN-CULUS.

BUT...

GO... ...ED-WARD.

COME ON, ED.

?

WHAT DO YOU MEAN?

IT'S NOT MUSTANG LOSING THAT WORRIES ME.

STAY BACK, LIEUTENANT.

CRACKLE
KRIK
SNIK
KRIK

AS A SIGN OF MY RESPECT, I'LL FIGHT YOU USING MY TRUE STRENGTH.

CRUNCH

RRRRRR RRRRRR RRRRRR

SO I SEE... YOU'VE BEEN HUNTING FOR HUGHES'S KILLER ALL THIS TIME.

WHAT A LOYAL FRIEND YOU ARE.

SNIK
SNIK
SNAK

FZT

DON'T SAY I DIDN'T WARN YOU!!

IT'S NOT EASY TO HOLD BACK IN THIS FORM!

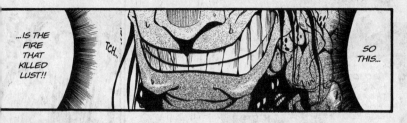

...IS THE FIRE THAT KILLED LUST!!

TCH...

SO THIS...

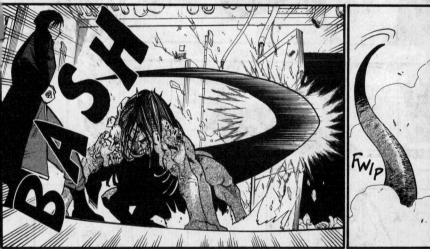

BASH

FWIP

VWOOM

KLATTA

KLUNK

WHAM

STOP!!

DASH

GWOON GWOON

I'VE GOT A SINKING FEELING IN THE PIT OF MY STOMACH...

I DON'T BLAME YOU.

BWOOP GLOOP

THIS PLACE SURE IS CREEPY.

THESE TUBES ARE LIKE VEINS.

GWOON

THIS WAY!

I THINK WE'RE CLOSE!

GWOON GWOON

GWOON GWOON

LIKE AN ENORMOUS WRITHING MASS OF *PEOPLE*...

DOES THAT MAKE SENSE?

I'M SENSING AN IMPOSSIBLY LARGE SOURCE OF LIFE ENERGY COMING FROM THAT DIRECTION.

LIFE ENERGY?

THAT SOUND...

RRUMBL

NOT REALLY, GIRL, BUT I DO GET *CREEPY*.

I HOPE WE DON'T ENCOUNTER THE ENEMY IN A PLACE LIKE THIS...

SCAR.

I NEED TO TALK TO YOU.

AS ONE WHO WAS ONCE DRIVEN BY VENGEANCE, I KNOW WHAT HE'S FEELING.

ABOUT THE FLAME ALCHEMIST?

SOONER OR LATER THOSE FLAMES OF HIS WILL BURN AWAY HIS VERY SOUL.

THAT MAN...

SHOW YOURSELF, ENVY!!

IF YOU DON'T COME OUT, I'LL FILL THIS WHOLE BUILDING WITH FIRE!!

BOOM

GRR...

LOOM

I'M NOT LETTING YOUR FLAMES ANYWHERE NEAR FATHER'S ROOM!

DASH

LIKE HELL YOU WILL!!

...ROY.

HEL- LO...

THERE YOU ARE...

NOW'S MY CHANCE...

HAH HA!! HE FLINCHED !!

FOOM

YOUR MOCKERY IS ONLY ADDING OIL TO THE FIRE!!

SON OF A...

YOU DIDN'T EVEN HESITATE TO ATTACK YOUR BEST FRIEND!

HUGHES IS DEAD!!

HE'S GONE!!

DAMMIT... I HAVE NO CHOICE...

FWOOM

I HAVE TO SUCK IT UP AND ENGAGE HIM UP CLOSE!!

HIS FLAMES ARE TOO POWERFUL TO USE IN CLOSE PROXIMITY TO HIMSELF.

HAVE A TASTE OF YOUR OWN FLAMES--

BZAP

SKKID

AAAAH!

JAM

GAAH!

NOT MY EYES AGAIN!

SIZZZZ

IT GOT AWAY AGAIN.

TCH!

FW UMP

FW UMP

WHERE COULD ENVY BE...?

!

GRIN

KLAK
KLAK KLAK

KLAAK

KLAAK

KLAAK

KLAAK

KLA...

KLAK

KLAK

KLAK

VAM

CHAK

...!!

WHO?

WHO DO YOU THINK YOU'RE POINTING THAT GUN AT?

WHAT ARE YOU DOING?

DON'T MAKE ME LAUGH.

...CALLS ME RIZA WHEN WE'RE ALONE.

THE COLO-NEL...

310

SO THAT'S HOW IT IS BETWEEN YOU TWO?

TCH!

I LIED.

NOW, THIS IS THE PART WHERE YOU DIE.

THANKS FOR TAKING THE BAIT, ENVY.

WHA...?

KLAK
KLAK

KLAK
KLAK
KLAK

KLAK

CRACKLE
CRACKLE

RRGH.

HUF

HUF

HUFF

HUF

HUF

WHAT ARE
YOU DOING
TO MY
PRECIOUS
SUBORDI-
NATE?

KLA...

DON'T BE RECKLESS, LIEUTEN-ANT.

I SAID I WOULD TAKE CARE OF IT.

BZZT

ZABOOM

YOU DARE TO LOOK DOWN ON ME ?!

HU-MAN SCUM !

BZT

CHAK

WEEZ...
HUFF...

....?

WHAT'S THE MEANING OF THIS, LIEUTEN- ANT?

LOWER YOUR GUN.

I HAVE NO INTENTION OF LETTING YOU DIRTY YOUR HANDS.

ONE MORE FLAME AND IT'S OVER.

I'LL TAKE IT FROM HERE, SIR.

THAT'S ENOUGH, COLO- NEL.

PLEASE PUT DOWN YOUR HAND.

I CAN'T OBEY THAT ORDER, SIR.

FULL-
MET-
AL...

HAND
IT
OVER
!!

322

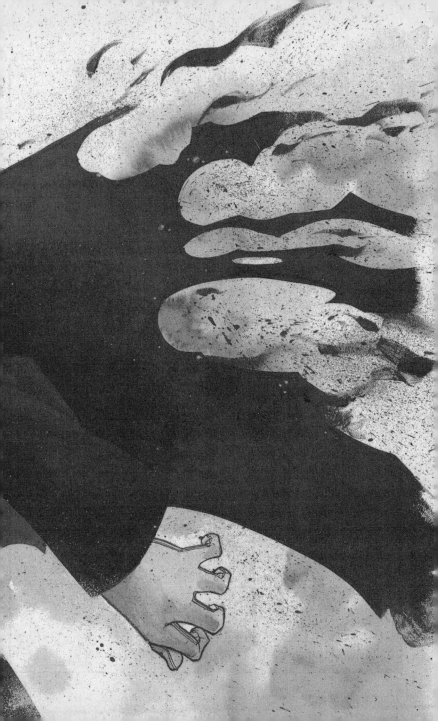

Chapter 95
Beyond the Inferno

FULLMETAL
ALCHEMIST

CRAP! I CAN'T TAKE OVER HIS BODY!

OH YEAH! THIS GUY'S RIGHT ARM IS AUTO-MAIL.

CHOMP

CHOMP CHOMP

THAT THING NEEDS TO DIE AS PAINFULLY AS POSSIBLE FOR WHAT IT'S DONE!

HAND IT OVER.

I SAID NO.

IF YOU DON'T, I'LL INCINERATE YOUR ARM RIGHT ALONG WITH IT!!!

HAND IT OVER, FULL-METAL!!!

GO AHEAD AND TRY!!!

I'LL TAKE YOU ON!!!

WITH A FACE LIKE THAT, HOW DO YOU EXPECT TO LEAD THIS COUNTRY?!!

BUT FIRST, TAKE A GOOD LOOK IN THE MIRROR!!

ISN'T THAT WHAT YOU'VE BEEN FIGHTING FOR, COLONEL?!!

OR WILL YOU SUCCUMB TO YOUR RAGE AND FALL TO THE LEVEL OF A BEAST?

THAT'S YOUR OTHER OPTION.

HEY!

AS LONG AS WE SHARE THE SAME ENEMY, I WON'T TRY TO STOP YOU.

I HAVE NO RIGHT TO STAND IN THE WAY OF SOMEONE ELSE'S VENGEANCE.

...I WONDER WHAT KIND OF WORLD CAN BE CREATED BY A BEAST HIDING IN THE SKIN OF A PERSON?

BUT...

I'LL FINISH IT OFF.

BUT I HAVE NO INTENTION OF LETTING IT LIVE EITHER.

I WON'T LET YOU KILL ENVY, SIR.

YOU MUSTN'T TAKE THAT PATH!

IF YOU WANT TO SHOOT ME, GO AHEAD.

BUT WHAT WILL YOU DO AFTER I'M DEAD?

...I WILL ERASE MY LIFE, ALONG WITH THE SECRET TO FLAME ALCHEMY THAT'S LED GOOD MEN TO MADNESS.

AFTER THIS BATTLE IS OVER...

I HAVE NO INTENTION OF LIVING ON ALONE.

SNAP

BOOM

...

I CAN'T ALLOW THAT.

LOOK AT ME...

SCOLDED BY A CHILD...

PREACHED TO BY MY FORMER ENEMY...

I'M NOT LOSING YOU TOO.

...AND WORST OF ALL, DRIVING YOU TO CONSIDER SUCH A THING.

LOWER YOUR GUN, LIEUTEN-ANT.

WHAT A FOOL I'VE BEEN.

I'M SORRY.

....!

SLUMP

PLOP

YOU WERE THE MOST HONEST PERSON HERE!

WHAT IS THIS, SOME CONTEST TO SEE WHO CAN BE THE NICEST?

I'M GONNA THROW UP!!

YOU WEREN'T A FOOL!

...AND LISTEN TO YOUR INSTINCTS!

YOU HUMANS SHOULD JUST DROP THE PRETENSE OF KEEPING THE MORAL HIGH GROUND...

AND YOU, RUNT!

SCAR KILLED THE PARENTS OF YOUR LITTLE GIRLFRIEND, RIGHT?

RIGHT ?!

COLONEL MUSTANG!

SCAR WAS TRYING TO KILL YOU, WASN'T HE?

SCAR WAS ALSO THE ONE WHO KILLED HER, WASN'T HE?!

OH YEAH! AND THE GIRL IN EAST CITY, WHOSE BODY WAS COMBINED WITH THAT OF A DOG!!

THANKS TO ME, YOU GOT TO MURDER A LOT OF PEOPLE, DIDN'T YOU, LT. HAWKEYE?!!

HA HA HA !!

AND THAT WAR IN ISHBAL THAT WAS STARTED BY ME, ENVY!!

CRAWL ON THE GROUND LIKE WORMS !!

WHAT A GROUP WE HAVE HERE!! KEEP HATING, CRYING AND KILLING EACH OTHER AS YOU WRITHE IN MISERY!!

TWO OF THE MOST EFFICIENT KILLERS IN THE GENOCIDE OF YOUR PEOPLE ARE RIGHT HERE IN FRONT OF YOU! NOW'S YOUR CHANCE!!

SCAR !!

ISN'T THAT RIGHT, SMALL FRY?!!

THERE'S NO WAY YOU INSECTS CAN LIVE PEACEFULLY TOGETHER!!

SCAR!!!

MUSTANG!!!

HAWKEYE!!!

WHY...?

...

ENVY...

YOU'RE...

DAMN IT!!!

WHY?! WHY?!! WHY?!!!

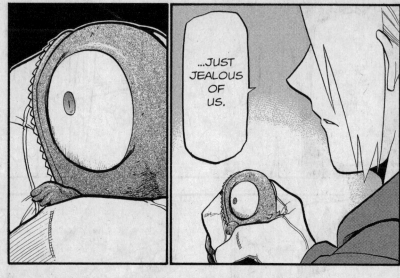

...JUST JEALOUS OF US.

HUMANS ARE SUPPOSED TO BE SO MUCH WEAKER THAN YOU HOMUNCULI, BUT NO MATTER HOW OFTEN...

...WE GET BEATEN DOWN...

...BECOME DISCOURAGED...

...LOSE OUR WAY...

...AND EVEN IF WE KNOW THAT IT'S FOR SUPERFICIAL REASONS...

...WE KEEP FIGHTING ON.

...COME CLOSE TO FALLING...

WE FIND STRENGTH IN EACH OTHER.

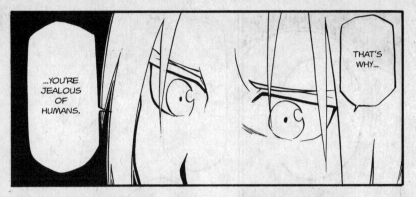

...YOU'RE JEALOUS OF HUMANS.

THAT'S WHY...

SHUV

DON'T TRY TO ES-CAPE!

WRIG...

HEY...

UNNGH...

WRIG WRIG WRIG...

KRAK

SNAP

WRIG WRIG

CHOMP

YEOW!!

YOU IDIOT! IF YOU TRY TO FORCE YOURSELF FREE...

PLOMP

SQUIP

HEH HEH...

SQUIG...

HEH...

341

WAIT.

CHAK

IT DOESN'T KNOW WHEN TO GIVE UP...

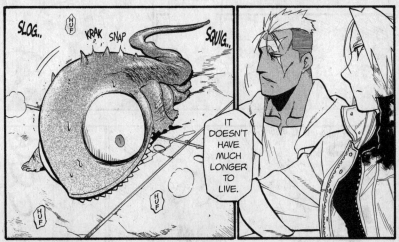

SLOG...

HUF

KRAK SNAP

SQUIG...

HUF

HUF

IT DOESN'T HAVE MUCH LONGER TO LIVE.

TO BE REDUCED TO THIS FORM...

HOW HUMIL- IATING...

HEH. HEH HEH...

342

...BY MERE HUMANS.

PANT

PANT

PANT

PLOP

TO BE MOCKED BY YOU WORMS !

AND WORST OF ALL...

...THE MOST PATHETIC, INSIGNIFICANT ONE OF YOU...

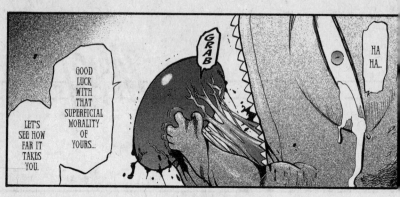

GRAB

HA HA...

GOOD LUCK WITH THAT SUPERFICIAL MORALITY OF YOURS...

LET'S SEE HOW FAR IT TAKES YOU.

SPLOOT

ZSHH

ZSHH

ZSHH

SQUISH

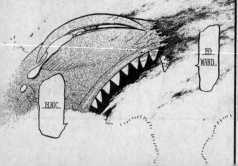

...ELRIC...

ED... WARD...

GOOD-BYE...

ZAAASH

THE COWARD.

IT TOOK ITS OWN LIFE.

GURG...
GURG...

346

A SQUAD!

C SQUAD! WHAT'S WITH THIS HOLE?!

BZZT FZZT

BZZT

YOU'RE JUST IN TIME! GIVE US A HAND!

ALL RIGHT, BUT MAKE IT QUICK.

WE HAVE URGENT ORDERS TO EXECUTE MAJOR GENERAL ARM-STRONG.

WHAT A MON-STER...

WHOA... ITS WOUNDS ARE HEALING!!

EVERYONE UP HERE LOOKS LIKE THEY WERE BLUDGEONED TO DEATH...

WHAT THE HELL IS GOING ON?

HRMH!!

THWOCK

EYAAAAAAH!!

GRAH

BULLETS HAVE NO EFFECT ON THEM!!

SEVER THE UPPER JAW!!

THAT WAY, AT THE VERY LEAST, WE WON'T BE CHEWED TO DEATH.

SL

ICE

THE ARM-STRONG MANSION IS COM-PLETELY DE-SERTED!

THERE'S NO ONE HERE!

SO THIS IS WHERE THOSE BASTARDS ASSEMBLED THEIR TANK!

KREE...

DAMN IT...

...RETURN FIRE!!

ALL TROOPS...

I WILL TAKE FULL RE-SPONSI-BILITY!!

CENTRAL COMMAND, MAIN GATE ARTILLERY...

IF WE WAIT FOR THAT, WE'LL LOSE THE GATE!!

BUT, SIR! WE HAVEN'T FINISHED EVACU-ATING THE CIVILIANS YET!!

KABOOOOM

?!

GACHANK

YOU WERE REALLY GOING TO OPEN FIRE IN THE DIRECTION OF THE CIVILIAN SECTOR?

DO YOU WANT THAT TO BE BROADCASTED ON THE RADIO TOO?

SNIK

360

HOW DID YOU GET IN HERE?

THOSE UNIFORMS-- YOU'RE BRIGGS MEN!!

FUNNY STORY. WE GOT A GUY HERE WHO USED TO WORK IN HQ. YOU SEND PEOPLE TO BRIGGS YOU WANT TO FORGET, BUT HE CERTAINLY REMEMBERED HOW TO FIND YOU GUYS.

STRIDE STRIDE STRIDE STRIDE

ON THE CON- TRARY, IT WASN'T HARD FOR HER AT ALL.

ALSO, WE HAD A LITTLE HELP FROM SOMEONE WHO MADE A TUNNEL HERE ALL THE WAY FROM THE CIVILIAN SECTOR.

WHEN SOMEONE ASKS, I USUALLY SAY, "I'M A HOUSE- WIFE."

WH... WHO WAS IT?!

THAT'S IMPOS- SIBLE !!

CALL ME OLD- FASHIONED.

Fullmetal Alchemist 23 End

Prologue

PEACE DIPLOMATS ARE ON THEIR WAY!!

A TRUCE HAS BEEN DECLARED!! THE SOUTHERN BORDER WARS ARE OVER!!

EXTRA, EXTRA!!

...THAT HIS HIGHNESS, PRINCE CLAUDIO OF AERUGO, WILL BE MAKING AN OFFICIAL STATE VISIT TO AMESTRIS!

FOR YEARS, EACH NATION HAS FOUGHT THE OTHER TO EXPAND ITS BORDERS.

AERUGO-- AMESTRIS'S NEIGHBOR TO THE SOUTH...

Amestris

Aerugo   Ishval

THE SECOND SOUTH-AREA BORDER WAR BEGAN IN RESPONSE TO THE AERUGO GOVERNMENT'S INVOLVEMENT DURING THE ISHBALAN CIVIL WAR.

THE ISHBALANS, A MINORITY ETHNIC GROUP, WERE GIVEN WEAPONS AND INTEL BY THE AERUGO GOVERNMENT IN ORDER TO MAXIMIZE AMESTRIAN LOSSES, BUT IN THE END, THE ISHBALANS WERE LEFT TO FEND FOR THEMSELVES.

YEAAH!

WHILE THAT WAR IS OVER, THERE IS SOME ANXIETY ABOUT RETALIATORY VIOLENCE FROM ISHBALAN TERRORISTS.

HIS HIGHNESS WILL BE TRAVELING IN A PRIVATE TRAIN COMPARTMENT AND IS SCHEDULED TO ARRIVE TOMORROW MORNING, SIR.

CRUMPA

...THIS CURSED HISTORY ?

DO PEOPLE BE-LIEVE...

EVERYONE! MAKE SURE TO GIVE HIS HIGHNESS A WARM AND MUSCULAR WELCOME!

YES, MASTER ALEX!

I TRUST THAT PREPARA-TIONS FOR THE WELCOMING FESTIVITIES ARE GOING SMOOTHLY ?

YES, SIR. ALL SECTORS OF THE CITY ARE ON TRACK.

...BIG BROTHER.

SEE YOU SOON...

CHUGA

CHUGA

CHUGA

CLAUDIO, THE PRINCE OF DAWN, IS ABOUT TO MAKE A FATEFUL VISIT TO AMESTRIS.

PARDON ME, YOUR HIGHNESS.

NOK NOK.

CHUGA

CHUGA

CHUGA

THERE ARE MANY WHO WELCOME HIM, SOME WHO ARE WARY OF HIM AND A FEW WHO WOULD PLOT AGAINST HIM.

...PRINCE CLAUDIO.

WE WILL BE ARRIVING IN AMESTRIS SHORTLY...

CHUGA

CHUGA

FULLMETAL ALCHEMIST
PRINCE OF DAWN

NOW...

...THERE'S NO ESCAPE.

HOW WILL IT GO DOWN?!

FULLMETAL ALCHEMIST 23

STRONG!!

SPECIAL THANKS to:

Jun Tohko

Noriko Tsubota

Kori Sakano

Masashi Mizutani

Haruhi Nakamura

Manatsu Sakura

Coupon

Kazufumi Kaneko

Teru Miyoshi

Yota Arao

My Editor, Yuichi Shimomura

AND YOU!!

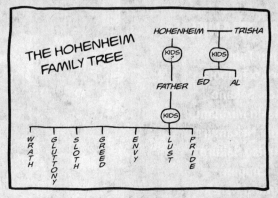

WHICH MEANS...

...IS THIS HOW THINGS COULD BE?

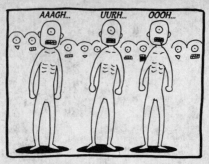

I recently found out that the typesetter is a relative of mine.

—*Hiromu Arakawa, 2009*

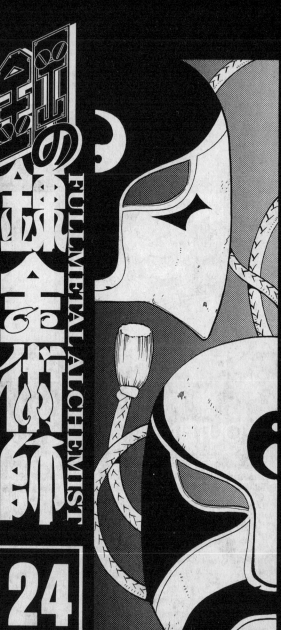

鋼の錬金術師

FULLMETAL ALCHEMIST

HIROMU ARAKAWA

荒川弘

24

■ アルフォンス・エルリック

Alphonse Elric

■ エドワード・エルリック

Edward Elric

■ アレックス・ルイ・アームストロング

Alex Louis Armstrong

■ ロイ・マスタング

Roy Mustang

OUTLINE
FULLMETAL ALCHEMIST

Using a forbidden alchemical ritual, the Elric brothers attempted to bring their dead mother back to life. But the ritual went wrong, consuming Edward Elric's leg and Alphonse Elric's entire body. At the cost of his arm, Edward was able to graft his brother's soul into a suit of armor. Equipped with mechanical "auto-mail" to replace his missing limbs, Edward becomes a state alchemist in hopes of finding a way to restore their bodies. Their search embroils them in a deadly conspiracy that threatens to take the innocence, if not the lives, of everyone involved.

As the "Day of Reckoning" approaches, Central City has become a war zone! On one side, the Homunculi and the military leaders who have sold out their country for power; on the other, a ragtag alliance of rebel soldiers loyal to Major General Armstrong of Briggs and Roy Mustang, Ishbalan refugees and, of course, the Elric family. Even the Elrics' former teacher, Izumi Curtis, has joined the fight! But deep beneath Central City lies the leader of the Homunculi, the Dwarf in the Flask, aka "Father." The original Homunculus is about to get a long overdue reunion…

鋼の錬金術師
FULLMETAL ALCHEMIST

CHARACTERS
FULLMETAL ALCHEMIST

■ セリム・ブラッドレイ（プライド）

Selim Bradley (Pride)

■ スカー

Scar

■ オリヴィエ・ミラ・アームストロング

Olivier Mira Armstrong

■ キング・ブラッドレイ

King Bradley

■ スロウス

Sloth

■ ヴァン・ホーエンハイム

Van Hohenheim

CONTENTS

Chapter 96
Two Strong Women

FULLMETAL
ALCHEMIST

WHIRR

KABOOOOOOM

DOOOM

CEASE FIRE!

CEASE FIRE!

CALL OFF THAT TANK!

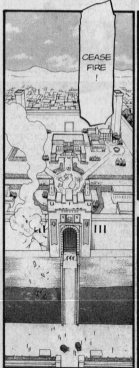

CEASE FIRE!!

CEASE FIRE!

CENTRAL COMMAND IS NOW UNDER THE CONTROL OF BRIGGS SOLDIERS.

THIRTEEN PRISONERS INCLUDING BRIGADIER GENERAL KLEMIN HAVE BEEN DETAINED.

I RE-PEAT...

RRGH!

...CENTRAL COMMAND IS LOCKED DOWN AND UNDER BRIGGS' CONTROL.

SO ALL OF THAT TANK FIRE WAS JUST TO DROWN OUT THE SOUND OF THE TUNNELING!

SOLDIERS OF CENTRAL CITY, DO NOT OPEN FIRE OR OTHERWISE INTERFERE WITH BRIGGS TROOPS OR COLONEL MUSTANG'S SQUAD.

URGH!

ANY EFFORT TO DO SO WILL RESULT IN KLEMIN'S HEAD BEING SEPARATED FROM HIS BODY!

GRIN!!

YOU GOT IT, BUB.

WHAK

BAM

THOMP

POW

GAK

BAM

WHAT ?!

I COULDN'T HEAR ALL THAT!

?!!

CENTRAL COMMAND HAS BEEN CAPTURED BY THE BRIGGS TROOPS, SIR!

WHAT HAP-PENED ?!

HUH ?!

AND BRIGADIER GENERAL KLEMIN'S BEEN TAKEN PRISONER!!

OOOOOOH

THIS BUILDING IS INFESTED WITH ONE-EYED, PALE-SKINNED HUMANOID CREATURES.

NOT ONLY ARE THESE THINGS HARD TO KILL, BUT THEY FEED ON HUMAN FLESH.

IS BUCCA-NEER THERE? PUT HIM ON!

KA-CHAK

AYE, AYE!

WHATEVER HAPPENS, DO NOT OPEN THE GATES!!

EXTER-MINATE THEM ALL WITHIN THE CONFINES OF THE HEAD-QUARTERS BUILDING ITSELF!!

WE CAN'T LET A SINGLE ONE OF THESE CREATURES GET LOOSE IN THE CITY!!

WHAT'S GOING ON? WHERE'S KLEMIN?!!

WH-WH-WH...

BAM

WE'LL SET UP A TEMPORARY HQ HERE!!

WE HAVE TO ASSUME THAT THE COMMAND CENTER HAS FALLEN TO THE ENEMY!!

KLAK

KLAK

THE PRESI-DENTIAL OFFICE!!

KLAK

KLAK

KLAK

JUST GET THROUGH THIS CRISIS AND...

THE PRESI-DENT'S CHAIR.

GULP...

388

MAJOR GENERAL! WHAT THE HELL ARE THESE THINGS?!

THEY'RE STILL SPAWNING!

THEY WERE MADE BY IMPLANTING HUMAN SOULS INTO ARTIFICIAL BODIES.

SOLDIERS WHO HAVE NO FEAR OF DEATH.

AN ARMY OF IMMORTALS.

GIVE ME A BODY...

FLESH...

FLESH...

GIVE IT TO ME...

FLESH...

SHRIP

KRAK

SHRIP

NO DOUBT YOU SOLDIERS WOULD END UP LIKE THIS IF HIGH COMMAND HAD THEIR WAY.

....!!

URG...

GUH GUH GUH

GLOG SLOG

IMPOSSIBLE! IT SHOULD BE DEAD!!

IT CAN STILL MOVE?!

GASP!

THEN I'LL JUST HAVE TO KILL IT AGAIN!!

WHOOM

...TOO MUCH...

...WORK...

SLOG

NNGH...

DY-ING IS...

THWOMP!

GRRRRRR...

...WAIT.

ITS AIM IS AS POOR AS EVER !

394

TUG
TUG
TUG

TUG

HOLD ON TIGHT!!!

KREE

KREE KREE

TUG TUG

TUG TUG

TUG ⟶ TUG

MAJOR! GENERAL! YOU HAVE TO GET OUT OF HERE!!

WE'LL CLEAR A PATH FOR YOU!!

HURRY, THIS WAY!!

A FEMALE GENERAL?

...WHO ARE YOU?

YOU MUST BE MAJOR GENERAL ARM-STRONG.

KRIK KRAK

YOUR SUBORDINATE ASKED ME TO LEND YOU A HAND.

THOUGH MY HUSBAND IS A THOUSAND TIMES A BETTER MAN THAN YOU'LL EVER BE.

THOSE MEDDLING DERELICTS!

GRAB

GUSH

SHLOOP

ER...

IT
CAN
STILL
MOVE...
?

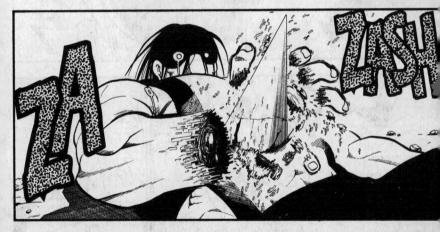

ZA

ZASH

FSH ZSHH

ZSHH

FSHH

HUH
?

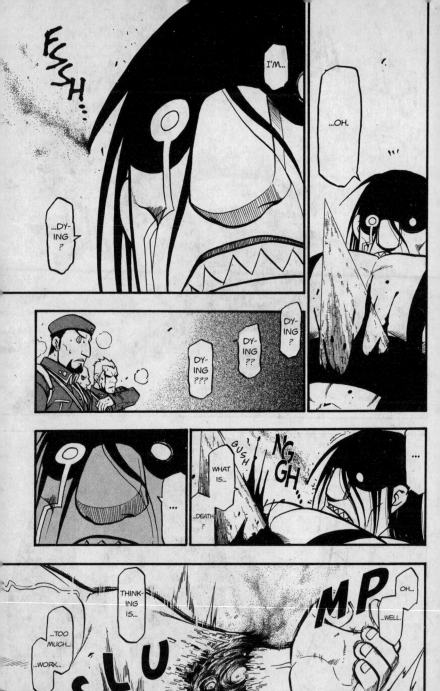

PHEW

MA-
JOR
!

PLOP

ZASHA

I DON'T KNOW WHO YOU ARE OR WHERE YOU'RE FROM BUT THANK YOU FOR YOUR HELP.

YOU'RE WEL-COME!

SORRY, BUT I NEED A BIT OF REST.

YES, MA'AM! LEAVE THE REST TO US!

NO, NO, NO. I'M JUST A HOUSEWIFE AND AN ALCHEMIST!

ME?

I'M GUESSING THAT YOU'RE A MARTIAL ARTIST OF SOME RENOWN...

I'M GUESSING THE ELRIC BROTHERS ARE INVOLVED IN THE BATTLE?

OF COURSE.

THEY'RE AROUND HERE SOME-WHERE.

THEN YOU MUST BE IZUMI CURTIS!

THOSE BOYS WERE MY STU-DENTS.

YOU KNOW THE ELRIC BROTHERS, DON'T YOU?

HEH HEH...

YOU CAN'T EXPECT US ADULTS TO STAY IDLE WHILE THERE ARE KIDS OUT THERE FIGHTING FOR THEIR LIVES!

I'M PER-FECTLY FINE!

LET ME GIVE YOU A HAND, BIG SISTER...

SHALL WE TAKE CARE OF THE RE-MAINING DOLL SOLDIERS?

HEY, HEY! YOU NEED TO REST!

WE ARE IN YOUR DEBT!

WELL, IN THAT CASE, YOU CAN COUNT ON OUR HELP.

THE YOUNG WILL INHERIT THE FUTURE, BUT RIGHT NOW WE ADULTS BEAR THE BURDEN OF THE PRESENT...

SO LETS SHOW THE NEXT GENERATION HOW IT'S DONE!

BUT DON'T GET YOUR HOPES UP.

APPARENTLY, I'M ONE OF THOSE "HUMAN SACRIFICES"...

SO I'LL FIGHT FOR AS LONG AS I CAN, BUT I'VE GOT TO MAKE MY EXIT...

...BEFORE THE BIG BADS COME FOR ME.

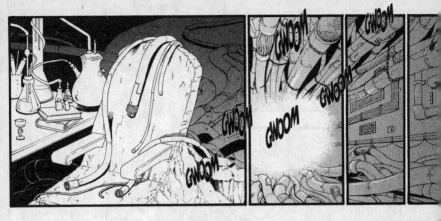

...

SO DOUR. IS THAT ANY WAY TO GREET AN OLD FRIEND?

WHAT A BORE YOU'VE BECOME.

YOU USED TO BE SO FULL OF LIFE, OF EMOTION!

IT'S TRUE THAT ANY ONE OF THESE IN EXCESS CAN LEAD TO SELF-DESTRUCTION...

...BUT ON THE OTHER HAND, THOSE FLAWS ARE THE VERY THINGS THAT MAKE US HUMAN.

SO, WHY REMOVE THEM FROM YOUR-SELF?

LUST, GREED, SLOTH, GLUTTONY, ENVY, WRATH, AND PRIDE...

HU-MANITY'S SEVEN DEADLY SINS.

I DO NOT WISH TO BE HUMAN.

I WILL BECOME A PERFECT BEING.

WHOA ?!

VOOM

SQUEE

CUT IT OUT.

I'M NOT MUCH OF A FIGHTER, YOU KNOW.

BZAP

VOOM

WHOA!!

SO, YOU DON'T WANT TO BECOME HUMAN?

HUP.

HUP.

SKUP

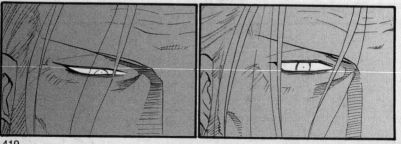

419

SHUNK

DWARF IN THE FLASK...

YOU LOST SOMETHING VERY IMPORTANT WHEN YOU GAVE UP YOUR EMOTIONS.

HUP

NOT MUCH.

BUT IT WAS THE ONE THING YOU NEVER THOUGHT TO DO.

A BEING WITH NO FEELINGS...

...CAN NEVER DEFEAT US SO EASILY.

Chapter 97
The Two
Philosophers

FULLMETAL
ALCHEMIST

THOSE ARE THE NAMES OF THE PEOPLE WHOSE SOULS YOU JUST TOOK INTO YOUR BODY.

BADUM

BADUM

THEY'RE COOPERATING WITH ME FOR THE SOLE PURPOSE OF DEFEATING YOU.

BUT THEY'RE NOTHING MORE THAN ENERGY!

YOU THINK IT'S IMPOSSIBLE?

THE STONE HAS INDIVIDUAL PERSONALITIES WITHIN IT THAT ARE HELPING YOU?

I'LL ADMIT, DEALING ONE ON ONE WITH ALL THOSE TRAPPED AND ANGRY SOULS NEARLY DROVE ME INSANE.

CON- VERSE ?

YUP.

WHICH IS EXACTLY WHAT YOU NEVER DID.

BUT I HAD ALL THE TIME IN THE WORLD TO CONVERSE WITH THEM...

...THANKS TO THE IMMORTAL BODY THAT YOU GAVE ME.

...AND I'VE CON- VERSED IN DEPTH WITH ALL OF THEM!

THERE ARE 536,329 SOULS WITHIN ME...

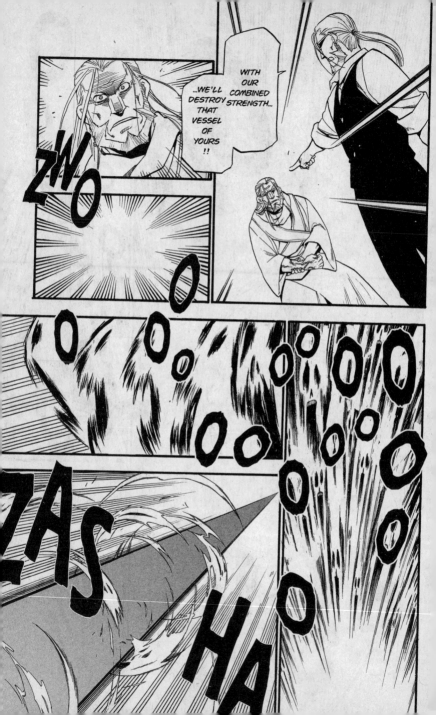

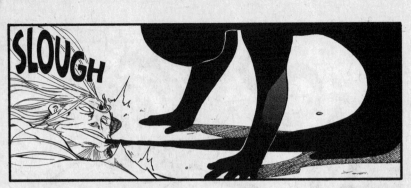

SLOUGH

SUU

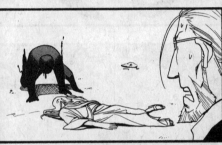

GLOOP...

GLOO...

GAPE

VIP

SLUUURP

ZU

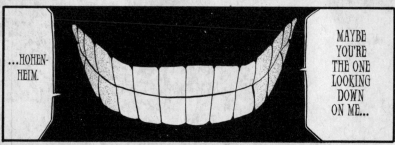

...HOHEN-HEIM.

MAYBE YOU'RE THE ONE LOOKING DOWN ON ME...

ZU ZU ZU ZU ZU ZU

YOU HUMANS AREN'T THE ONLY ONES WHO HAVE EVOLVED!

ZU ZU ZU ZU

YES, SIR!

NOW, WE'LL TAKE THE FRONT GATE!

SLAM

THWAAK

BAM
WHAK
POW

UH... SAVE SOME FOR US?

THOK

WHOMP

BAM

442

WHY IS THIS HAPPENING?!

BLAM BLAM

BACK!

BACK!

I WASN'T MEANT TO DIE IN A PLACE LIKE THIS!!

STAY BACK! STAY BACK!

DID THAT MAN LIE TO US?!

I THOUGHT YOU ALL WERE MADE TO TAKE ORDERS FROM US!!

SMACK

AAAIEEE!!

GRAAA!!

IF YOU DO I'LL SEE THAT YOU ARE WELL REWAR--

G-GUARD ME!!

...

I, UH, I DON'T KNOW WHO YOU ARE BUT NICE WORK!!

OH...

RRGH?!

SOCK!

SPLAT

FWUMP

RA-TAT-TAT-

TAT-TAT...

THIS "MAN" YOU WERE TALKING ABOUT.

WHAT CAN YOU TELL ME ABOUT HIM?

MA-
JOR
GEN-
ERAL.

HAVE
A
LOOK.

WHAT A
MESS
THE
PRESI-
DENTIAL
OFFICE
IS IN.

WHOA...

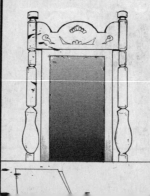

SHALL
WE SET
UP YOUR
COMMAND
CENTER
HERE,
MA'AM?

BLACK SQUAD HAS COMPLETED SUPPRESSION. NORTH GATE HERE.

THIS IS THE WEST GATE. BRIGGS WHITE SQUAD HAS COMPLETED THE SUPPRESSION OF THIS SECTOR.

YELLOW SQUAD HERE. WE HAVE SEIZED THE ARMORY.

EAST GATE HAS BEEN SUPPRESSED! BLUE SQUAD HERE.

UNDER NO CIRCUMSTANCES SHOULD ANY OF THE GATES BE OPENED UNTIL EVERY LAST DOLL SOLDIER IS EXTERMINATED.

CAPTAIN!

BUCCANEER SQUAD, PLEASE STANDBY.

448

NINETY PERCENT OF CENTRAL CITY HEADQUARTERS IS NOW UNDER OUR CONTROL.

THANK YOU FOR ALL YOUR HARD WORK, MAJOR GENERAL ARM-STRONG.

WE DID IT.

AW, CRAP!

THE COLONEL DIDN'T MAKE IT IN TIME.

WE WON!

HELLO EVERYONE, I'M BACK.

IT SEEMS THERE'S BEEN A LOT OF COMMOTION WHILE I'VE BEEN GONE.

I ORDER ALL CENTRAL CITY SOLDIERS, WHO ARE STILL ABLE TO FIGHT, TO AID ME.

I WILL NOW PERSONALLY ASSUME COMMAND AND ELIMINATE THE REBELS.

MURMUR MURMUR MURMUR MURMUR MURMUR MURMUR

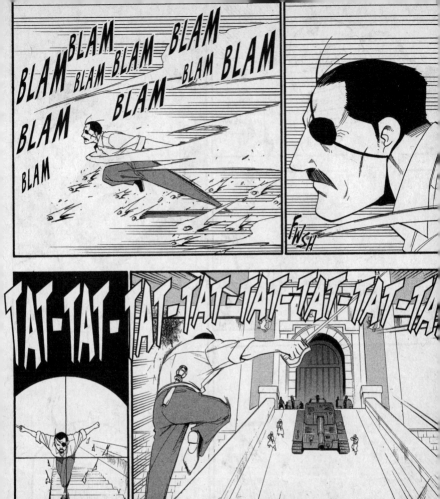

455

456

CAP-
TAIN
BUCCA-
NEER
!!

OPEN
THE
GATE.

KLAK

KLIK

KLAK

YOUR
MASTER
HAS
RETURNED.

WHAT
ARE
YOU
WAIT-
ING
FOR?

462

SHAKA SHAKA SHAKA

...FALMAN.

OPEN THE GATE...

I'M SORRY, COLONEL MUS- TANG...

SWP

BUT I...

DRIP

.DROP

CHAK

I THINK I'VE REACHED THE END OF MY ROAD...

YOU DON'T CRY WHEN YOU'RE SHOWING OFF YOUR BRAVERY.

HEY, BUB.

CHINK

NOW, STEP ASIDE AND LET ME SHOW YOU HOW MANLY COURAGE IS DONE.

I CAN STILL FIGHT!

WHAT'S THE MATTER, BRADLEY?

GETTING CARRIED AWAY BY YOUR EMOTIONS IS DOWNRIGHT IDIOTIC.

HE'S EXACTLY RIGHT!

RIDICU-LOUS.

THAT'S WHAT'S KNOWN AS RECKLESS COURAGE.

SNIK

GREED... YOU SHOULD'VE JUST STAYED QUIET AND RAN AWAY.

SORRY, BUT MY GREED KNOWS NO LIMITS.

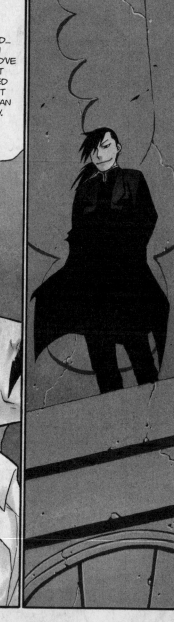

THAT'S WHY I WANT YOUR LIFE TOO...

...WRATH.

Chapter 98
Greed Without Limits

FULLMETAL
ALCHEMIST

DID YOU HEAR? PRESIDENT BRADLEY IS BACK!!

WE SHOULD REGROUP AND TAKE BACK THE COMMAND CENTER!

REALLY?!

BUT THE BRIGGS TROOPS AREN'T OUR ONLY ENEMY, YOU KNOW.

DIDN'T YOU SEE THOSE PALE MONSTERS?

HAH! JUST WHAT THOSE BRIGGS BASTARDS DESERVE!

I HEARD HE TOOK OUT THAT BRIGGS TANK AT THE FRONT GATE ON HIS OWN.

NO, THEY WERE ATTACKING THE BRIGGS TROOPS TOO.

COULD THEY BE BIOLOGICAL WEAPONS FROM BRIGGS?

WHERE DID THOSE THINGS COME FROM?

THEY DON'T DIE, EVEN WITH THEIR HEADS CUT OFF.

WORD AROUND TOWN IS THAT YOU DIED IN THAT TRAIN EXPLOSION.

HOW DID YOU SUR-VIVE?

...ARE YOU ?

WHO...

LONG TIME NO SEE, WARRANT OFFICER FALMAN.

I'M A 2ND LIEUTENANT NOW!

YOU'RE THE GUY WHO PUT ME UP IN THAT CRAPPY APARTMENT!

HEY, AREN'T YOU...

...LIN YAO?

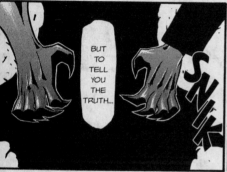
BUT TO TELL YOU THE TRUTH...

SNIK

I'LL GIVE YOU A HAND.

I OWE YOU A DEBT FOR GIVING ME FOOD AND SHELTER.

I'M ONLY DOING IT FOR PERSONAL REASONS!

TMP TMP TMP TMP TMP TMP

HEH HEH...

MY BUDDY INSIDE TAUGHT ME HOW TO FIGHT YOU.

CIRCLING AROUND TO MY BLIND SPOT AGAIN?

IS THAT SO?

THEN LET'S TRY THIS.

WHOOM

SHING
KLANG
SHING
KLANG
WHOA...
KLANG
YIKES!
SHING
KLANG

WHAM
IS HE IN TROUBLE?!
ARGH
HE'S ON THE DEFENSIVE NOW!

BLAM
FIRE, FIRE!!
AID HIM!!
BLAM
UH-OH!
BLAM BLAM
TMP
WHY YOU--!
WHO
FSH
OSH

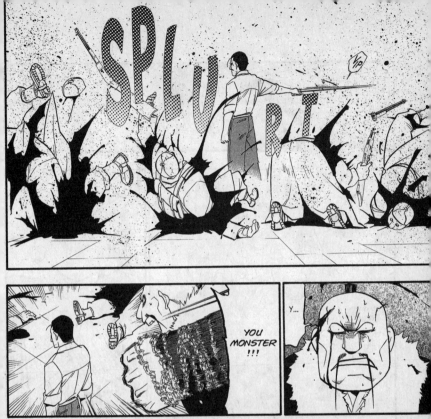

Y...

YOU MONSTER !!!

SHUNK

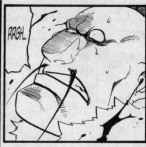

YOU HAVE SOME STRONG ABS.

DON'T BE SO RECKLESS, YOU FOOL!!

CAPTAIN!!

GOOD GRIEF.

BUT GOOD JOB ANYWAY!!

HEH

NO MORE RELYING ON YOUR PRECIOUS SWORD SKILLS.

KASHIIIING

NOT MY WEAPON OF CHOICE, BUT THESE WILL DO.

SKREECH

TCH!

VRM VRM VRM VRM VRM

HE'S PRESENTLY ENGAGED IN COMBAT WITH AN UNIDENTIFIED ASSAILANT.

YES, SIR.

KLAK KLAK KLAK

THE PRESIDENT HAS RETURNED?!

YES, SIR.

UNDERSTOOD.

FOCUS ON THE REBEL SOLDIERS.

DON'T INTERFERE WITH THE PRESIDENT'S BATTLE.

CHAKA CHAKA CHAKA

WE'RE TAKING BACK THE FRONT GATE.

GET YOUR MEN ARMED.

486

DOOM

MOVE, MOVE !!

IT TAKES TIME TO SET UP, SIR!

HEY, CAN YOU OPERATE THIS THING ?!!

THE CENTRAL TROOPS ARE MOUNTING A FRESH ATTACK !

TMP TMP TMP TMP TMP TMP

NOT GOOD !!

WHAM

NOT BAD, OLD MAN.

WHOA...

BUT IT'S THAT AURA THAT ALLOWED ME TO TRACK YOU.

IT MAKES ME SICK TO SENSE YOUR VILE AURA COMING FROM HIS HIGHNESS'S BODY...

HUMPH... YOU'RE GREED RIGHT NOW, AREN'T YOU?

THAT'S KING BRADLEY.

WHO IS THIS MAN WHO FACES OUR COMBINED STRENGTH, YET REMAINS UNSCATHED?

OH HO!

AT LAST WE MEET FACE TO FACE.

SO...

CLENCH

YOU'RE THE BASTARD WHO CUT OFF MY GRAND-DAUGHTER'S ARM!

RADIO CAPITAL

FIRST LADY BRADLEY!

UH HUH...

REALLY?!

THE PRESIDENT HAS RETURNED!

HE'S ALIVE!

!!

IS SELIM SAFE?!

HE'S NOT HURT, IS HE?!

TCH!

THAT WE DON'T KNOW YET.

OH... OH!

I'M SO GLAD...

APPARENTLY, THE PRESIDENT IS AT THE CENTRAL HQ, WHERE HE IS LEADING AN ATTACK AGAINST THE BRIGGS REBELS.

YES... I JUST WISH I KNEW THAT SELIM IS SAFE AS WELL.

I'M SO GLAD TO HEAR THAT YOUR HUSBAND IS SAFE.

I GUESS WE PIN IT ALL ON MAJOR GENERAL ARMSTRONG, THEN?

GREAT.

I HEAR THAT HER SQUADS ARE SLAUGHTERING CENTRAL CITY TROOPS!

I WONDER HOW MANY OF THE HIGH COMMAND SHE HAS UNDER HER INFLUENCE?

YOU MEAN THE FEMALE GENERAL WHO RECENTLY ARRIVED IN CENTRAL?

IF THE PRESIDENT IS FIGHTING THE BRIGGS TROOPS, THAT MUST MEAN MAJOR GENERAL ARMSTRONG IS THE MASTERMIND BEHIND THE COUP.

HUH?

SO WE'RE NOT SAFE HERE, EITHER.

CONSIDERING HOW HE'S BEEN USING THE FIRST LADY ALL THESE YEARS, HE'LL PROBABLY WANT TO TIE OFF THAT LOOSE END.

KLAK

KLAK

KLAK

KLAK

NEVER UNDER- ESTIMATE A HOMUN- CULUS.

SO HE WAS ALIVE...

DON'T FIRE!

WE WANT TO TALK!

GU SH

FOR
CRYING
OUT...

TAT
TAT

BLAM

BOOM

499

LET ME GET THIS STRAIGHT.

YOU'VE BEEN PLOTTING TO SACRIFICE COUNTLESS INNOCENT MEN AND WOMEN SO THAT A HANDFUL OF OFFICERS COULD ATTAIN IMMORTALITY AND RULE THE WORLD?

IN FACT, HE WAS CREATED TO HELP US BRING IT ABOUT.

IS PRESIDENT BRADLEY AWARE OF YOUR PLAN?

OH, YES.

500

WELL? WHAT ARE YOU LOT GONNA DO?

OOPH!!

SMACK

SMACK

THOK

OOPH!!

YOU HEARD THE MAN. IS THAT THE FUTURE YOU WANT?

YOU GONNA LET HIM GET AWAY WITH THAT?

IT'S NOT TOO LATE TO JOIN US. I'LL TALK TO THAT MAN AND--

A-ALL OF YOU, YOU HAVE TO LISTEN TO ME!

AS FAR AS BELIEVING IN SOMETHING, I REALLY DON'T KNOW *WHAT* TO BELIEVE IN ANYMORE.

BUT HON-ESTLY...

...I HAVE TO FOLLOW THE ORDERS OF MY SUPERIOR OFFICERS.

I... I'M A SOLDIER SO...

BELIEVE IN YOURSELF.

SEARCH YOUR HEART AND CHOOSE A PATH THAT YOU WON'T BE ASHAMED OF.

MINE AS WELL.

...MY FAMILY'S OVER THERE.

MINE TOO.

I HAVE A GIRL-FRIEND OUT THERE.

SNAP

SIR...

THIS IS OUR ANSWER.

TING TING POFF

HOW'S THE SITUATION?

NOT GOOD.

CENTRAL CITY TROOPS ARE GAINING GROUND AT EVERY GATE.

COME IN, COMMAND CENTER.

OVER.

YES, MA'AM.

WE'VE LOST CONTACT WITH OUR ALLIES IN YOUR VICINITY.

IT'S LIKELY THAT YOU'RE SURROUNDED BY CENTRAL CITY TROOPS.

WHAT'S YOUR CURRENT LOCATION, MAJOR GENERAL?

I'M IN THE PRESIDENTIAL OFFICE.

I SEE.

...UNDER-STOOD.

IF YOUR LOCATION COMES UNDER ATTACK, RETREAT THROUGH THE HOLE YOU CAME OUT OF.

DO NOT WAIT FOR ME.

IT'S ONLY A MATTER OF TIME BEFORE THE CENTRAL CITY TROOPS STRIKE THIS LOCATION TOO.

THE ENEMY IS RE-GROUPING.

WELL THEN...

CLICK...

506

OOOO

WHICH MEANS...

THAT'S STRANGE.

GWOOM

DOWN IT IS.

I COULDA SWORN IT WAS THIS WAY...

OR WAS IT THAT WAY...?

GWOOM

GWOOM

HMM..

GWOOM

GWOOM

MAY, WHERE ARE YOU?!!

HEY!

THE ONLY REASON THIS IS HAPPENING IS BECAUSE I CAME BACK TO BAIL YOUR SUCKY BUTT OUTTA TROUBLE!

I NEVER ASKED YOU TO COME.

ARE YOU LOST, FULLMETAL?

LO--

...

YEAH RIGHT!! IF SCAR AND I HADN'T BEEN THERE TO HELP YOU, YOU WOULDA GONE OVER THE EDGE!!

IT WAS THE LIEUTENANT WHO PULLED ME BACK TO MY SENSES.

DON'T BE SO FULL OF YOURSELF.

SCAR...

I WANTED TO THANK YOU.

THEY'RE TOO LOUD. THE ENEMY WILL FIND US.

SIGH...

508

...I WANT TO THANK YOU FOR MAKING THE COLONEL SEE REASON.

AS AN ISHBALAN, I KNOW YOU MIGHT RESENT THIS, BUT...

...HE WAS FINALLY ABLE TO GET RID OF HIS DEMONS.

BE- CAUSE OF YOU...

I DON'T NEED YOUR GRATI- TUDE...

...

THANKS.

TUG

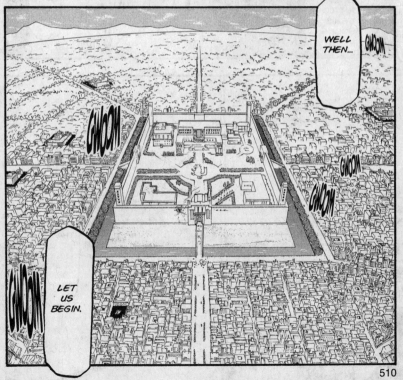

510

Chapter 99
Eternal Rest

FULLMETAL
ALCHEMIST

BOOM

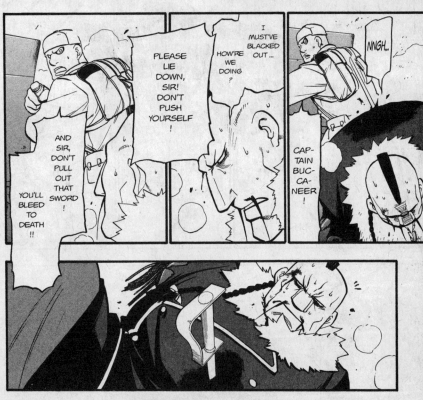

PLEASE LIE DOWN, SIR! DON'T PUSH YOURSELF!

AND SIR, DON'T PULL OUT THAT SWORD! YOU'LL BLEED TO DEATH!!

HOW'RE WE DOING?

I MUST'VE BLACKED OUT...

NNGH...

CAPTAIN BUCCANEER!

OH, RIGHT...

YOU PUT YOUR OWN LIFE AT RISK FOR THE SAKE OF THOSE WHO YOU CAN'T BEAR TO ABANDON.

THE SAME THING HAPPENED WHEN I CUT OFF THAT GIRL'S ARM.

DON'T SAY THAT!

DO YOU WANT ME TO STOOP TO KING BRADLEY'S LEVEL?!!

MY PRINCE... MY DAYS OF FIGHTING ARE OVER. JUST LEAVE ME...

HE'S WILLING TO ABANDON THE PEOPLE OF HIS OWN COUNTRY.

I'LL NEVER BE LIKE HIM!

FOO!!

KOFF KOFF GACK

THEN, HE MUST BE DEFEATED...

A MAN UNWORTHY TO RULE...?

...

DON'T TALK! JUST REST!!

YES...

REST...

REST WOULD BE NICE.

UGH...

SMACK

HARDEN YOUR SKIN, GREED!!

PROTECT THE PRINCE'S BODY!!

MY PRINCE...

BECOME THE KING YOU ARE DESTINED TO BE.

?!

SNIK

SNIK

SNIK

THIS OLD MAN...

GUS

SHA

SPURT

PLIP

MY PRINCE...

I HAVE FAILED YOU...

I SACRIFICED MY LIFE...

...AND LEFT NOT A SCRATCH ON HIM!!

...BUT EVEN YOU CAN'T BLOCK AN ATTACK THAT YOU DON'T SEE COMING.

YOU MIGHT HAVE GODLIKE EYESIGHT...

OLD TIMER...

LET'S WALK THAT BASTARD TO HELL...

...TO-GETHER.

GUSH

YES...

THAT'S KIND OF YOU...

NNGH...

WHACK

RM
RM
RM

RM
RM

RRRUUUMBLE

ME?

UM...

I GUESS YOU COULD CALL ME THE MAN WHO CREATED KING BRADLEY.

WHO ARE YOU?

ALTHOUGH MY LEFT EYE ROTTED AWAY IN THE PROCESS, I GAINED SUPERHUMAN STRENGTH AND REFLEXES.

THEY INJECTED THE PHILOSOPHER'S STONE INTO MY BODY.

!

RRUMMB

SHP!

SO IT'S GOING TO COME DOWN TO THAT AFTER ALL, EH?

THEN, YOU LEAVE ME NO CHOICE.

TUG

...YOU'RE ON *THEIR* SIDE.

WHICH MEANS...

WHOOSH

GO, MY CHILDREN.

BUY ME A LITTLE TIME.

WHAK

WHAK WHAK

WHAT ARE THESE GUYS ?!!

WHOOM

DOLL SOL- DIERS...

?!

THEY ARE THE MEN WHO FAILED TO BECOME KING BRADLEY.

NO...

THEY WERE BROUGHT HERE AS INFANTS.

?!

THEIR MOVEMENTS ARE CLEARLY DIFFERENT FROM THOSE OF THE DOLL SOLDIERS!

BUT ONCE WE SUCCEEDED IN CREATING KING BRADLEY AFTER TWELVE ATTEMPTS, WE HAD NO FURTHER USE FOR THE OTHER CANDIDATES.

THEY ENDURED ALL MANNER OF TRAINING, HOPING TO BECOME THE FUTURE FUHRER-PRESIDENT.

538

...THE LEFT-OVERS.

THEY WERE THE ONES WHO NEVER TASTED THE PHILOSO-PHER'S STONE. IN OTHER WORDS, THEY ARE...

ACK

WH

THEY MAY NOT COM-PARE TO KING BRADLEY...

THESE MEN HAVE KNOWN NOTHING BUT COMBAT TRAINING FOR THE PAST SIXTY YEARS.

POP

TCH

DODGE

DODGE

VOOM

...BUT THEY'RE STILL DEADLY.

!!

FZZT
BZZT
FZZT
FZZT
BZZT
BZZT

THAT WAS JUST THE FIRST STAGE.

NOTH-ING MUCH.

WHAT THE HELL DID YOU DO ?!!

DO YOU KNOW HOW MANY GOVERNMENT-RUN ALCHEMY RESEARCH FACILITIES THERE ARE IN CENTRAL CITY?

NO...

FIVE.

IT USED TO BE CALLED LABORATORY NUMBER FIVE...

YEAH, THERE ARE FOUR OF THEM...

...FIVE APEXES ?!!

A TRANS-MUTA-TION CIRCLE WITH...

...IS A PERFECT CIRCLE THAT CONNECTS THE LABORA-TORIES ?!

CRACKLE

RACKLE

CRACKLE

COULD IT BE THAT THE CURVED TUNNEL BENEATH LAB NUMBER THREE...

!!

544

WHAT IN THE...?!

WHOA!

VWOOM

DASH DASH DASH DASH

WE NEED TO HURRY UP AND FIND A WAY TO GET UNDER-GROUND.

WHERE DID YOU LEARN TO DRIVE, YOKI!

DASH

DASH

SHUT UP!

JUST BE THANKFUL WE EVEN GOT THIS FAR IN A CLUNKER LIKE THAT!!

DASH

DASH DASH

THERE'S SMOKE COMING FROM CENTRAL HEADQUARTERS!

FLINCH

I HOPE HE'S DOING ALL RIGHT...

I WONDER IF THAT'S MUSTANG'S DOING?

WHAT'S WRONG, MR. HEINKEL?

SHUDDER SHUDDER SHUDDER SHUDDER

LEAP

Fullmetal Alchemist 24 End

Special Episode:
Fullmetal Alchemist, Wii: Daughter of the Dusk
Prologue

PRINCE CLAUDIO HAS ARRIVED IN CENTRAL CITY!!

CLAUDIO, PRINCE OF THE NEIGHBORING KINGDOM OF AERUGO, SHOCKED THE WORLD BY COMING TO AMESTRIS...

...ON A MISSION OF PEACE.

HIS DIPLOMATIC VISIT, WITH THE INTENT TO END THE WAR BETWEEN THE TWO NATIONS, HAS CREATED A STIR AMONG THE CITIZENS OF AMESTRIS.

※Wii is a registered trademark of Nintendo Inc.

THE CITY IS OVERFLOWING WITH FESTIVITIES HELD IN HONOR OF THE OCCASION.

EVEN NOW, THE CARNIVAL BEING HELD BEFORE THE SIGNING OF THE PEACE TREATY IS NEARING ITS CLIMAX.

DUSK HAS AR-RIVED.

YES...

NOW IS THE TIME TO BRING THE DARKNESS TO THIS PLACE.

FULLMETAL ALCHEMIST
Daughter of the Dusk

BIG
BROTHER
!!!

She's come to find something to believe in.
Coming soon to the Nintendo Wii

FULLMETAL ALCHEMIST 24

FROM CHAPTER 97.

SPECIAL THANKS to:

Jun Tohko

Masashi Mizutani

Coupon

Noriko Tsubota

Haruhi Nakamura

Kazufumi Kaneko

Kori Sakano

Manatsu Sakura

Kei Takanamazu

My Editor, Yuichi Shimomura

AND YOU!!

Hey! You're Reading in the Wrong Direction!

This is the **end** of this graphic novel!

To properly enjoy this VIZ graphic novel, please turn it around and begin reading from **right to left.** Unlike English, Japanese is read right to left, so Japanese comics are read in reverse order from the way English comics are typically read.

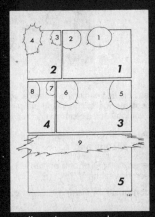

Follow the action this way

This book has been printed in the original Japanese format in order to preserve the orientation of the original artwork. Have fun with it!

FULLMETAL ALCHEMIST
3-in-1 Edition

VIZ Media Omnibus Edition Volume 8
A compilation of the graphic novel volumes 22–24

Story and Art by Hiromu Arakawa

Translation/Akira Watanabe
English Adaptation/Jake Forbes
Touch-up Art & Lettering/Wayne Truman
Manga Design/Julie Behn
Omnibus Design/Yukiko Whitley
Manga Editors/Annette Roman, Alexis Kirsch
Omnibus Editor/Hope Donovan

FULLMETAL ALCHEMIST vol. 22–24
© 2009 Hiromu Arakawa/SQUARE ENIX.
First published in Japan in 2009 by SQUARE ENIX CO., LTD.
English translation rights arranged with SQUARE ENIX CO., LTD.
and VIZ Media, LLC.

Printed in the U.S.A.

Published by VIZ Media, LLC
P.O. Box 77010
San Francisco, CA 94107

10 9 8 7 6 5 4 3 2 1
Omnibus edition first printing, July 2014

www.viz.com

I didn't get to draw Hughes and Lust here, but I guess everything turned out all right?

Recently, I realized that the characters I've been so casually drawing on the spine of the cover only consist of the ones that made it to the final arc of the story.

—Hiromu Arakawa, 2009

Born in Hokkaido (northern Japan), Hiromu Arakawa first attracted national attention in 1999 with her award-winning manga *Stray Dog*. Her series *Fullmetal Alchemist* debuted in 2001 in Square Enix's monthly manga anthology *Shonen Gangan*.